THRILL RIDE

A Million Miles. 2000 Shows. One Miraculous God.

Auny Gill

First Edition (pre-release)

Order additional copies by visiting www.brockgill.com.

Printed through Create Space (Amazon).

Library of Congress Cataloging-in-Publication Data: TBD

Gill, Auny.

Thrill Ride:

Includes bibliographical references. ISBN TBD 0692289372

1. Gill, Auny 2.Christian living 3. Biography

Printed in the United States of America
12 13 14 15 16 AAG 6 5 4 3 2 1

CONTENTS

ACKNOWLEDGEMENTS

First of all, I would like to thank my heavenly Father and Lord, Jesus Christ. Without Him, this book would not be written, because none of this would have happened without His intervention.

I would like to thank my dear husband, Brock. He has been such a support throughout the process of writing this book. He has given me the opportunity to have the adventurous life I've dreamed of. He inspires me to be a better person!

I would like to thank my sister, Kay Jones, my mom, Pam Baker, and my mother-in-law, Linda Gill, who read draft after draft of this book over the years and have helped edit and encourage me through the process.

Thank you, John Driver. Without all of your hard work in getting this book out, I would have given up long ago.

Thanks to our wonderful manager, Robert Noland, who keeps our ministry on track in many ways.

Thank you, Rod and Susan Riley, for being our faithful cheerleaders.

To everyone I wrote about in this book, thank you for sharing these times in life with me. I changed some of your names or did not list some of you by name, but you know who you are. Without your participation in my life, the book would have been incomplete.

Thank you to Jacob Henley for the awesome cover artwork and to Beth Jusino, my content editor. Also, thanks to the copy editors Audrey Jackson and Linda Gill.

I would like to give a special thank you to the ones who made this project a reality. Without your generosity, this book would not be possible: Addison Diamond, Nicka Howard, Jenny Lain, Sheila Shrader, Dora Ochoa, Rhonda Marple, Alma Lilley, Jennifer Swain, Red and Glenda Blanchette, Benji Varner, David and Kylie Knight, Claire Tyner, Amy Stansell, Preston and Pam Baker, Donnie Choate, Tiger Coffman, Nicole Blunt, Amanda McClanahan, Chris Pace, Lindsey

Davis, Lanny Donoho, Shannon White, Stephanie Skipper, John Driver, Grant Medford, Emily Kilbourn, Mary Brawner, Doris Godbey, Trent and Kay Jones, Cortney Harrold, Carlene Spruell, Deanna Meekins, Brian and Stephanie Britt, Heather Cartee, Stone and Britt Meyer, Roger and Linda Gill, Matt and Denise Shuff, Michawn Ebersole, Amber Thompson, Kathryn Garren, Ryan Reed, Robby and Jenny Poe, Kim Callender, Stephanie Day, Heather Monaghan, Max Sevier, Chip and Amanda Seagroves, Beth Patterson, Robin Pass, Earl and June Nelson, Tim and Edye Bisagnio, Phil and Jeanne Newberry, Teresa Giles, Davis and Janis Moulder, Garrett and Carrie Buell, BJ and Danielle Hunt, Harris III, Jessica Fletcher, Jody and Brandi Holloway, Brent Vanhook, Ben and Kara Glover, Elizabeth Hobafcovich, Pamela Hintz, Mandee and Cristi, Sean and Andrea Emory, Les and Patsy Clairmont, Haley Hays, Darrell Hawkes, Denzil Garretson, Josh Jordan, Joanne Hohenstern, George and Terae Reader, Jodi Vanderhoof, Dana and Tom, Kari McBee, Bethany Barr Phillips, all of our friends at JRA, Waylon and Tuesday Billings, Kimberly Diamond, Scott Humston and New Dimensions Evangelism, Jordan Smith, Kenny Avery, Kent and Ruby Skipper, Frank Shelton, Joe, Natalie, and Peter Nowell.

PROLOGUE

I had made it! I was finally sitting in the cart ready to go on my very first roller coaster. At 13 years old, I thought I was done being scared of everything. That was for kids. I was not a child. I was a teenager. As my hands gripped the bar in front of me and my knuckles began turning white, only one word could describe how I felt...terrified!

I had heard about the infamous "Space Mountain" for years. It was the biggest roller coaster in all of Disney World. Since I grew up in Florida, my family made the hour-long drive to the famous amusement park often. I always watched older kids in line for the roller coaster, but I was not able to go. Either I didn't reach the height requirement or the line was too long. My dad would say, "Maybe next time." Disappointment and relief flooded through me.

This time there were no more excuses. I was in the cart, already strapped in. I looked at my friend in front of me. Tiffany had been on Space Mountain many times before. She glanced back and gave me a reassuring smile. "You are going to love this!"

The cart lurched forward in a jerky fashion. My long brown hair flowed behind me as I was torpedoed into a dark room with a few neon lights. Suddenly I was unsure about this. I was not prepared to be in the dark. I couldn't see my hand in front of my face and the ride was much faster than I expected. Could I get off? Nobody would see me if I even could get anyone's attention to stop this scary train. There was no turning back now. I was stuck.

The cart whipped around a corner and then another corner and then stilled. I then felt myself being pulled upward in a slow motion. The only noise I could hear was the clicking of the train of carts ascending. Maybe the fast part was over. We slowed even more and then it happened! The cart propelled down, down, down at mach speed! There was a tingling in my stomach that rose up into my chest.

PROLOGUE

I ascended again with great acceleration, but instead of dropping, I was propelled sharply to the right for a while and then descended some only to take another sharp turn the other direction!

Every move was so unpredictable. I could not anticipate any turn because of the utter darkness. I had no control.

I was unaware of anyone else. The screams coming from people around me began to fade and all my senses were tuned into the way I felt.

A new sensation was flowing through me. It was exhilarating and addictive. The corners of my mouth turned up into a smile. Giggles bubbled up inside me until I could not contain them.

Suddenly, doors opened and I was shot through a tunnel with flashing colorful lights. I could see the back of Tiffany's head in front of me and remembered I was not alone.

After we exited the tunnel, our cart came to a jerky halt. I watched as Tiffany exited the cart. I quickly unbuckled my seatbelt and ran to catch up with her.

"Come on!" she said. "Everyone is waiting for us!" We were the last of our group to ride.

We exited out of the air conditioning and into the hot September sun. There, standing outside, were the rest of my youth group from church. I looked around at the girls and guys who were like family. All eyes were on me as Mrs. Godbey, our volunteer youth leader, said, "Well, what did you think?"

"I want to go on it again!" I exclaimed.

One of the older guys laughed saying, "I knew you would like it," as he patted my head in a big brother fashion.

"How did you know I would like it?" I asked.

"You are the adventurous type," was his reply.

A few years later, my family moved from Florida to Texas, and I attended a small Christian university there. In college is where I found the love of my life. The adventure really began when I met my husband.

It's a fabulous love story.

CHAPTER ONE
The Love Story

"Gideon replied, 'If now I have found favor in Your eyes, give me a sign that it is really You talking to me.'" Judges 6:17

It was August 23, 1997, when I slipped through the door of East Texas Baptist University's chapel. I saw many familiar faces at the "Back-to-School-Bash." A nervous energy ran through me.

My best friend, Gin, noticed my entry and ran down the aisle to me.

"Happy birthday!" I said giving her a hug.

"I am so excited about my party at Chili's after this!"

"I think more people are coming than ever before! I already called the restaurant to warn them," I said anticipating a great night. I was the unofficial party coordinator for my group of friends. Any excuse to celebrate was good enough for me.

"Are you glad this is your last year?" Gin asked, changing the subject.

"It's bittersweet," was my answer.

"Who knows how many more years I have to go? If I could just stick with a major, then maybe I could graduate this century!" she said rolling her eyes. "You are so lucky you came to college knowing exactly what you wanted to do."

She was right. I already knew the graduate school I would attend the following fall so that I could get my degree in counseling. It had been my plan for several years.

"Hey, what's going on with Adrian?" she asked, referring to my first boyfriend.

"We broke up," was all I said. A sad feeling of something lost came across my heart. Even though I knew Adrian was not the right one for me, it was nice to have someone who cared for me differently than anyone else in the world.

"Again? Well, it's his loss! You deserve a guy who will treasure you and cannot live without you," she said matter-of-factly.

The student government's president walked up to the microphone center stage.

"Ooh, I have to get backstage! It's about to start," Gin said running back down the aisle.

I sat with some friends as Gin's band took the stage. Looking around at the people gathered, I had mixed emotions about my senior year. I came to school not knowing another soul. Now, I felt like I had many relationships that would last a lifetime.

After the show was over, I quickly rounded up a car load of people and headed to Chili's. They seated all thirty-two of us at a long table in the back. I sat at one end next to Gin.

Scanning the table to see who was in attendance, my eyes rested on a tall, thin guy with crazy, blonde hair sitting at the opposite end of the table whom I didn't recognize. There was something about him that commanded my attention. He was laughing with some of the people sitting around him. His laugh was so infectious that I began to chuckle.

"What's so funny?" Gin asked me.

"I just thought of something humorous," I mumbled.

I decided that would be a good time to walk around to the other side of the table to talk with my friend, Brian, who happened to be sitting next to the guy who had so instantly piqued my interest. I walked up to Brian and we exchanged hugs and briefly discussed our summers. "Do you remember my friend, Brock, who was here a couple of years ago? We are both from Saline, Louisiana," Brian said as he motioned to the intriguing guy with the gregarious laugh.

Recognition set in as I realized this was the famous Brock Gill. Although he looked a little different from what I had remembered, I had seen this guy my first year of college. I knew of him that year but had never had the opportunity to meet him. He had a reputation for having spontaneous church services in the open-air quad on campus and baptizing people in the fountain there. After my freshman year of college, his sophomore year, he disappeared from school.

"No, I don't believe I do," I lied.

"This is Auny. She's cool," Brian said.

Brock took my hand and shook it in a formal fashion. As he did, our eyes locked. It seemed as if his clear blue eyes were looking past my face and straight to my soul. His look was so intense that I began to feel self conscious.

"Auny is it?" Brock asked as he dropped his hand.

"Well, my name is Andrea but my sister couldn't say it when she was little so she called me 'Auny.' Then, my parents and eventually all my friends began calling me 'Auny.' Even when I came to school here four years ago, I introduced myself as 'Andrea' to people. By Christmas, everyone was calling me 'Auny.'"

I secretly scolded myself for rambling as I tended to do when I got nervous. Sometime in my digression, Brian began talking with someone sitting near him. Brock was the only one hearing my little name explanation. He listened so intently that I felt like we were the only two people in the room.

"Maybe 'Auny' fits you better than 'Andrea' does," Brock said.

"Maybe so," I said sheepishly. "Well, maybe I will see you around sometime."

"I'm sure you will," Brock said.

Brian grabbed my arm as I started to walk back to my seat. "You should come over to our house on Saturday night. We are having a party."

"Your house?" I asked.

"Brock and I are renting a house on Hope Circle off campus."

"I'll be there!" I said with a smile.

****

"This is the place," I told Gin as we pulled up to an old house tucked back in a cul-de-sac.

"You look nice by the way. You being all dressed up wouldn't have anything to do with Brock Gill living here, would it?" Gin turned in my direction.

"I'm not all dressed up!"

"You're wearing makeup."

"I wear makeup!"

"Not that often," Gin said with a smile as we got out of the car and headed toward the door.

"Look, I'm more intrigued by him than attracted to him. After everything I've heard about him, I find Brock rather mysterious."

"I heard he joined a cult the last two years while he was gone," Gin said.

"I'm sure that's just a rumor."

Light poured through the windows and I could hear voices inside. I knocked on the door.

A few seconds later Brock opened it and smiled. "Hello, Auny," he said accentuating my name. I introduced Gin and we walked into the spacious living room lined with couches. People were mingling around. A couple of them shouted their hello's over the voices. Gin joined a group of people standing in the kitchen just beyond the living room.

"I like that fish tank," I said pointing toward it hanging over the fireplace.

"The best room in this house is the 'cool room.'" Brock leaned his tall body down to speak so that I could hear him over the chatter.

"Take me to it." I responded.

I followed him through a beaded curtain into a room adjacent to the living room. Immediately the noise from the other room muffled and I was in darkness.

I heard Brock fumbling around and then a click. A black light came on lighting up my light-colored shirt as well as glow in the dark stars on the ceiling.

Couches lined the walls of this small room and foil was covering the windows so no light could come in.

"This is a cool room," I said looking around.

"Brian's going to add another fish tank in here, too. He's really into fish these days."

"It must be nice to live in a house," I said looking around the room. "This will be my fourth year in a dorm."

"Why can't you move off campus?"

"They will take away my scholarship if I do, and I cannot afford this school without that scholarship."

"Well, you can come to this house any time you want to," Brock said with a nod. "I'm serious! We never lock our door. Just come on in."

"I may just do that," I said.

Some others from the party joined us in the "cool room" and we all sat down and talked. People filtered in and out of the room all night, but Brock and I stayed there sitting next to each other talking and laughing for hours.

Later that night, when we were back in our dorm, Gin said, "You and Brock seemed really cozy tonight. Were sparks flying?"

"Brock is great. In some ways, I feel like I've known him all my life.

Like he's family or something, but there were no sparks," I answered.

"Oh, well, you have to have sparks," Gin said disappointedly.

"But he's going to be a great friend. I can tell!" I said meaning it.

****

In the days following, Gin was busy with her band, so I found myself alone much more than I had been the previous years when Gin and I were inseparable.

One night, I decided to take Brock up on his offer and go to his house. I knocked twice but nobody answered. I tentatively pushed open the door and began yelling for Brian or Brock.

"In here," I heard from the other room. I walked past the living room and into the small kitchen to find Brock sitting at the table.

"Hey!" he said with delight as he saw me.

"Are any of your roommates here?" I asked.

"No, I'm the only one home right now. Come and sit. Want something to eat?" he asked gesturing toward his plate of Raman noodles.

"No thanks. I already ate. Can I ask you something, though? Where did you go in your two year summer break?" I asked as I plopped down on the seat next to him.

"I went to Texarkana and worked at a sawmill."

My jaw dropped and I said, "I cannot see you as a sawmill worker."

"I wasn't very good at it. This scar from a chainsaw is proof of that," he said pointing to a jagged stitched marking along his left elbow.

"Ouch," I said wincing at the thought of the pain it ensued.

"I had a lot of time to pray while I was working at the mill. Ten hours a day with earplugs gave me plenty of time to talk with God about what He wanted me to do with my life."

"Did He give you any direction?"

"Yes," was all Brock said.

"Well, what was it?" I asked with anticipation.

"It's a crazy story," Brock said.

I leaned in eager to hear it.

He explained that the youth pastor at the church where he was ministering took him to a magic shop. The man behind the counter did a simple card trick, and it sparked something in Brock that had not been extinguished since. He bought a trick from him and practiced it over and over. He couldn't put it down.

The Lord told him that He wanted him to create an illusion show in order to share the gospel with people. He thought he was going crazy at first because this seemed so illogical. After a few sleepless nights, he realized God was serious about it.

Shortly after that, he went on a twenty-one day fast. He used this time to pray about how this unusual ministry should go and what he needed to do to get started. In this time, the Lord told him to stop dating. He would marry his best friend and she would be his assistant onstage. God also directed him to quit the sawmill and come back to school.

That's what brought him here. He worked the night shift at a hotel for the first three weeks he was back. One day, he felt the Holy Spirit coaxing him to quit the hotel job and focus on his new ministry. He was obedient, and by noon the next day, he had booked three shows without so much as a business card promoting him.

"I got the call from God, and then, I got the physical calls to do shows," he said. "That's how I knew this ministry was really from God."

I admired his passion and vision. Immediately, I knew this guy was going to do great things for the kingdom of God.

"What about you?" he asked. "What's your story?"

I told him about when I was at youth camp the summer after eighth grade. People were going to the altar during a service. I felt myself being drawn to move. As I sat knelt down at the steps leading to the stage, my camp leader came up to me and whispered, "I think you are being called into the ministry."

I looked at her and repeated what I felt the Lord was impressing deep down in my soul. "One day my husband is going to be in the ministry and I am going to be very involved."

My dad was a pastor and my mom was at every church event. She went with him to visit people in the hospital. She cried with ones who had lost a family member while Dad gave words of encouragement and strength. They made a wonderful team. Doing ministry alongside my husband was not just a calling, but a dream of mine.

"Is that why you came to this school? There are lots of guys planning on being pastors here." Brock interjected bringing me back to the present.

"No, I came to this school because the Lord told me to come here. One day in high school, I was sitting in the guidance counselor's office and I saw a bulletin board with large posters from several state schools. In the bottom corner was a tiny bumper sticker that said, 'East Texas Baptist University.' At that moment, the Holy Spirit whispered, 'That's where I want you to go.'"

"And just like that, you came," Brock said.

"Just like that. It was the only school I applied to, because I was certain this was where the Lord wanted me," I said with confidence. "I am majoring in psychology and plan to be a child psychologist."

"So, you are going to be a children's counselor and a pastor's wife," Brock said as he took his bowl to the sink. "What if your husband is a traveling minister like a worship leader or an evangelist?" he asked while washing his dish.

"No, I couldn't be married to someone who traveled. He would be out on the road having adventures without me."

"What if you traveled with him?"

"Then, I couldn't be a child psychologist."

"I see your point." He dried his hands and looked in my direction. "This is a total change of subject, but can I show you some of the tricks I'm working on? You could be my guinea pig."

"Sure," I said as Brock began to demonstrate what he had learned. I was very drawn to his passion for the Lord and desire to share the message of Jesus Christ.

After that night, I often found myself at Brock's house. I felt at home there.

Many times Brock and Brian would have people over for a barbecue. Brock was fond of cooking and he was good at it. As guests entered the house, he would say, "We have all kinds of food...chicken, ribs, burgers, whatever you want!" I quickly learned that I needed to bring my own side dishes, because these bachelors only cared about the meat!

The entertainment was always illusions by Brock. He was a natural at it! Brock was so entertaining... funny and charming.

I began hanging out with Brock, Brian, and their friends most of my free time. Whenever a group of us would go out to eat, Brock and I would literally be five steps in front of everyone else. We were both fast walkers. No need to waste time in life on a silly thing such as walking to and from locations. We would be telling a server in the restaurant how many were in our party before everyone else was even out of their cars. Because of this, we ended up sitting next to each other and talking a lot wherever we went.

We always spoke so easily together. Our friendship was natural. I felt like I could tell him anything, and I did. He would share his plans and what was happening with his newfound ministry. I would discuss my plans after I graduated. We even talked about people we were interested in dating.

It wasn't a romantic relationship. I could talk with him like I used to talk with Gin. Since she was so busy, Brock stepped into the place of being my best friend.

We had much in common. We were both preachers' kids. We both had a desire to seek after the Lord's will for our lives. We were both thrill seekers, and we both longed to have fun.

One evening the following spring, the phone rang in my dorm room.

"Want to come over and play?" Brock asked after I picked up. It was what he usually said when he called.

I smiled as I replied, "Sure!"

When I opened the door to his house, I saw a girl sitting on the couch in the living room.

"Hello," I said to the stranger.

Brock ran into the room from the kitchen and grabbed my hand and began dragging me back toward the door.

He glanced at the girl and said, "We are going to the movies. See ya!"

He pushed me out of the door and closed it quickly behind us. He let out a sigh of relief.

"Brock! Not again! That girl totally thinks I'm your girlfriend," I said rolling my eyes.

"I'm counting on it! She just showed up and cooked dinner for me. Then, I couldn't get rid of her," he said shrugging as we got into my car.

I handed him the keys and said, "You are too encouraging to girls."

"What?" he said bewildered.

"Look, I thought you were into me that way when I first met you, too. You seemed too eager to see me and you listened so closely. Then, I noticed that you did that with everybody. You genuinely love being around people and enjoy whoever's company you are in. That's a wonderful quality to have, but it can be misleading with some girls."

"So, I should be rude?" Brock asked.

"Not rude, just back off a little."

"I could try."

"Yes, try," I said. "How am I going to meet a guy if everyone thinks that I am your girlfriend?"

"You are not my girlfriend," Brock said looking at me. "You are just my favorite person."

"That's sweet of you, Brock. You're my favorite person in life right now, too."

I looked over at him as he drove and smiled, "But you're still in trouble for using me to get rid of another stalker girl!"

After the movie, we went back to his house and he took a seat on one of the couches while I sat on the floor with my legs out in front of me.

"It's starting to get warm again. Every spring I itch to be back in Florida. The sand feels so good in between my toes," I said closing my eyes as I pictured myself there.

"It's only an eight-hour drive to Pensacola," Brock said bringing me out of my daydream.

"Really?" I asked.

He had been there a few times before and enjoyed it. "When do you want to go?"

"Tomorrow," I said grinning at him.

"Okay, let's do it!" Brock said.

I laughed thinking he wasn't serious.

"I'm not joking. Let's just go!"

Brock, myself, and a few other friends loaded up in his van the next day and took off to Pensacola Beach, Florida.

We took other spontaneous trips to New Orleans, Louisiana and South Padre Island, Texas that year. Brock would drive the group of us and I would be the navigator.

Once, while we were driving, I told him that we were looking for a place called "Mount Blossom." As we passed an exit reading "Flower Mound," I said, "That was it!"

Brock looked at me and said, "I thought you said Mount Blossom?"

My face turned beet red as embarrassment set in. I was self conscious about very little, but this was an area where I felt insecure. I got my words confused often. Most of the time I would have the main concept but would be just a little off. Brock was an excellent communicator, so I figured something like this would be offensive to him.

I could not flee to the bathroom like I used to do back in junior high after I said something embarrassing. I was stranded in the passenger's seat of Brock's van with no comeback.

I waited in anticipation to see how he would respond to my blunder. After several grueling seconds, he turned his face back toward the road and howled in laughter!

I did not like this reaction. My face remained red, but this time it was out of anger. I did not say anything, but since I am so expressive, my irritability was written all over my face.

"Now, Auny," Brock said. "Isn't this another part of your charm?"

He was referring to the time when he noticed how clumsy I was on a daily basis. When he brought it to my attention, I had simply smiled and said that it was part of my charm.

This was a different matter, though. I was so transparent with facial expressions that I could not hide any of my feelings, but was not so great with my words.

"I think the fact that you referred to 'flower mound' as 'mount blossom' is extremely charming," Brock continued.

"You do?" I asked as I began to calm down.

"Yes," Brock assured me. From then on, he thought it was so funny when I got things mixed up that he would never correct me. He would only begin laughing uncontrollably after I stated something backwards or inside out or whatever happened to tumble out of my mouth. To this, I would respond, "What did I say wrong?"

I began to accept this part of my personality to be just what Brock said it was...part of my charm.

Brock had such a quick wit. I, on the other hand, would tell a joke and wonder why nobody got it. Then, I would realize that I mixed up the punch line and it no longer made sense. Brock taught me that if I could learn to laugh at myself, I could be humorous without even trying.

****

After graduating from college in May of 1998, Gin and I moved into a one-bedroom apartment in the next town over and I began grad school. I was taking classes at night and working a full time job as a youth caseworker, working with troubled teens during the day. I did not have time for much else.

On occasion, I took the 30 minute drive to Brock's house to hang out. However, he was rarely there. He was completing his last year of school and doing his magic/evangelistic shows all over Texas every weekend.

The first Sunday night in November of that year, I was sitting in the living room of my apartment. Gin was out on the balcony talking on the phone. She was still going to college, so, unlike me, she had friends.

Grad school was not what I had anticipated. Everyone there knew exactly what they wanted to do, and they were serious about it. I, on the other hand, was beginning to have my doubts.

I had wanted to be a child psychologist since I read the book Cybil in the seventh grade. However, now that I was actually doing what I wanted by working with troubled teenagers, it was not as easy as I thought. One of the girls I was counseling didn't show up for our coffee date the previous week. I found out the reason was because she had attempted suicide the night before and was in a psychiatric hospital. As a counselor, you shouldn't bring your work home with you, but I couldn't help it. I saw this young woman's desperate face everywhere.

I got up to go to bed when I heard a knock at the door. Who could this be? We rarely had any visitors. I cracked the door open to try and see who it was.

Before I could even comprehend what was going on, the door flew open and I felt arms picking me up in a hug and twirling me around. Sheer exhilaration took over when I realized it was Brock. He stopped spinning but still held me so that we were face to face. We both froze. Since he was over a foot taller than I, we had never been eye to eye before. We were so close.

I felt like I was hitting the first drop on a roller coaster. Tingling in my stomach began to disperse to all parts of my body.

"Hi," Brock said as he lowered me back down to the floor. "I've missed you."

"Me too," I said believing how true that statement was. "What are you doing here?"

"I am on my way back from a show," he answered as we sat down on the couch.

"How did it go?"

"Auny, I cannot tell you how great these shows are going! God is moving in such a big way. It's working! I begin the show with half an hour or more of just sheer entertainment. Then, I use an illusion to illustrate the gospel. When I give them a chance to respond to Jesus, many are actually doing it! Tonight, during the invitation time, one guy went to the bathroom and wiped off the Marilyn Manson makeup he was wearing. It was a visual display of what was happening inside of him."

"I wish the kids I work with would go to your show. It's frustrating because I cannot talk about the one thing that my clients really need...a personal relationship with Jesus." I said still feeling discouraged about my career path.

"Maybe you should quit."

"Quit my job or grad school?"

"Both. If you don't feel empowered when you learn something new in class, or on a high after you have a good session with one of your clients, maybe you are not where you should be."

"I am not a quitter!" I said as my cheeks began to heat up. Why was I getting so defensive? He was only trying to help me. I ordered myself to calm down.

"Oh, I know that you are very determined, but that's not what I mean. What do you picture your life looking like in five years?"

"I will be married to a pastor of a church, and I will be a counselor," I said with a slight sharpness in my voice.

"Will you live in a house with a white picket fence?" Brock chuckled as he playfully punched me in the arm.

"Well, we will have a house. The fence would be bonus," I said softening.

"The girl that travels on a moment's notice and takes different routes home from work everyday doesn't strike me as a white picket fence kind of girl."

I let out a sigh from deep within as I thought about Brock's words. He was right. If I had a routine life, I would feel handcuffed. What if I was going the wrong direction?

Surely, the Lord had led my steps up until this point. He would let me know if I needed to take a turn. However, an uneasiness began to settle in me.

"Hey, what do you think about Alyssa?" Brock said breaking into my thoughts.

"Your new assistant?" I asked.

"Yeah, I kind of like her, but I wanted to know what you thought first."

My mind drifted back to the first time I met her at one of Brock's shows a couple of weeks before. She was a freshman with short, blonde hair and was so bubbly. Brock acted different around her. He cracked cheesy jokes and had a nervous laugh that did not sound genuine. Just thinking about it made me nauseous.

"She's cute, I guess," I answered looking down. "You are not going to ask her on a date are you? Remember what the Lord told you in your fast! You will marry the next girl you go on a date with."

"Whoa, Auny! I'm not that serious about her. I'm just interested. That's all," he said as he stood up. "I have to go. It's getting late and I have an eight o'clock class in the morning."

I reluctantly walked him to the door.

"Bye. Let's hang out more often." He gently bent down and kissed me on the cheek. A rush went from where his lips had grazed my face and extended all the way down to my toes.

When I shut the door, I shivered. I looked back to the spot on the couch where he was sitting. It felt so homey while he was here. Now, in his absence, I felt alone again.

And that kiss on the cheek! Brock had touched me before, held my hand on occasion or a little peck on the cheek, and I felt nothing.

Tonight was different. Something was beginning to awaken inside of me for the first time. Tonight, I felt sparks!

Four days later, I was driving home from my night class. The clock on the dash read 8:30. It had been a long twelve hours since I left my apartment that morning.

As a "Chicago" song began to play on the radio, I thought about that kiss Brock gave me. What if he would have kissed me on the lips? Why was I still having these crazy thoughts? How could a kiss on the cheek linger for four days?

I turned off the radio and began to pray out loud like I often did on my drives to and from school. This prayer was different.

"Okay, Lord. I'm having feelings, very romantic feelings, for Brock. However, he's my best friend...probably the best friend I've ever had. I cannot mess this up. The way I see it, either Brock and I are going to marry or we are going to stay friends."

I thought about that calling so many years ago. "My husband would be in the ministry and I would be very involved." Is Brock who the Lord had in mind? I had been to a few of Brock's shows. I had even played his sound cues for him on occasion. What if I could help Brock, be his assistant?

I thought about what my life would look like if I married him and we traveled the country doing illusion shows and sharing Jesus with people. I grinned as the image took root. It felt right.

I needed to be sure about this. It would only work if it was God's plan. I prayed for a sign from the Lord to indicate if He wanted Brock and me to get married. I laid down the fleece like Gideon in Judges 6. I asked the Lord to have Brock come over to my house that night on his own accord if the Lord wanted us to deepen our relationship. This would be my sign.

When I pulled into the parking lot of my complex, I half expected Brock's truck to be there. It was not.

As I walked up the stairs to my apartment, doubts began to form. It would take a miracle for Brock to drive all the way to my house this time of night on a Thursday. He had an eight o'clock class in the morning.

I had to get a grip on things. Brock was not there. He was not coming over; thus, I would not get my sign.

I walked through the door and saw Gin making dinner in the kitchen.

"Hey!" I called to her. "Have you checked the answering machine?"

"I forgot to," she said bringing her plate of food into the living room.

"We have two messages," I said as I hit the button.

Brock's voice filled the room. "Auny, I had a bad show last night and I really need to talk. Call me as soon as you get this."

The computerized voice indicated that the message was left at 8:32 a.m.

"I must have just missed his call this morning," I said.

After a series of beeps, the next message began. It was from Brock as well.

"I really need to see you. I am going to head over to your house right now." The computerized voice said, "8:30 p.m."

I jumped to my feet! "That was thirty minutes ago, exactly when I prayed that prayer!" I exclaimed.

"What prayer?" Gin inquired.

I looked at her and said with a calm confidence, "I am going to marry Brock Gill."

She looked up from her plate and nonchalantly said, "I could see that."

At that moment, there was a knock on the door.

"There he is. I'm going to go over to the neighbor's house for a while," she said as she rose from the couch. She patted me on the arm and said, "Let me know how it goes!"

She opened the front door allowing Brock to step inside as she exited carrying her plate of food.

He looked upset while I could not stop smiling. "You had a bad show?" I asked trying to sound more concerned. All I could think about was how I was going to let him know that we should get married.

We sat down on the couch next to each other. I purposely leaned in a little closer than I normally did. He rested his arm on the back of the couch and turned to face me. His knee brushed mine, and I gasped as his touch sent shivers down my spine.

He began to explain that the night before he had done the show and given an invitation and all went well. Then, things turned ugly. The pastor pulled him in his office and yelled at him that he was not teaching the gospel right.

"He said that if you don't know the exact date and time of when you said the sinner's prayer, you are not really saved," Brock said as his cheeks reddened.

"I told him that a prayer doesn't save you. Jesus does. You can begin your relationship with a prayer, but to say that it has to be a certain way and you must know the exact date and time of when it takes place is ludicrous. The point is not how but Who. We must realize that we are diseased with the curse of sin. We are desperate for a Savior. The only One who can take away the curse and provide a way to the Father in heaven is Jesus. We need to surrender our lives to Him."

"The pastor didn't believe that?" I asked.

"I guess not because he gave me an ear full in his office about how I said it all wrong. I think he was angry because some of his students were ready to really give their lives to Christ last night. They had said the 'sinner's prayer' when they were young but did not truly mean it until last night.

"Brian and Alyssa were at the show, but they didn't go into the pastor's office with me."

"Did you tell them about what the pastor said to you?"

"No, I could have told them on the way home. For some reason, the only person I wanted to talk to was you," he said as he looked straight into my eyes. "It was too late when I got home last night, so I called you as soon as I woke up this morning."

Excitement pulsed through my veins. Could the Lord have set this up last night knowing that I would make my request for a sign?

"Why do you think you wanted to talk to me? Brian's your best friend, and you said that you like Alyssa." I leaned in even closer so that our faces were almost touching.

"Wait a second!" Brock said as he stood up. "What's up with you? You are acting strange."

"I feel strange. Ever since you came over the other night, I've felt differently about you." I looked down at the ground. "I cannot stop thinking about you."

I paused gathering up nerve. "Do you have any romantic feelings for me?" I timidly asked without looking up at him. The question hung in the air for a few exasperating seconds.

He sat back down on the couch close to me and put his hand under my chin. He raised it up so that we were looking each other in the eyes. "Of course I do. There is not a day that goes by that I don't wish that we could be together, but we can't."

"Why not?" I asked as a tear slipped down my cheek.

Brock reached over and wiped the tear away. "You have your whole life planned out. You are going to be a counselor and you are going to marry a pastor. I cannot give you the picket fence."

"What if I don't want the picket fence anymore? Brock, we can make this work together."

"Well, I know that! You and I," Brock paused as he brushed a strand of hair from my face, "we can do anything together."

He cupped my face in his hands as he gently leaned down and kissed me on the lips. Fireworks shot through me! How could I spend so much time with this guy and not know that there were these deep underlying feelings?

"You know what I just remembered?" Brock said.

"What?" I mumbled, my head still in a fog from the kiss.

"During my twenty-one day fast, not only did the Lord tell me to stop dating. He told me that I would marry my best friend." He smiled down at me. "I met you two days after I broke that fast."

"And we definitely became best friends," I added as I smiled.

****

It was a warm, sunny day on May 8, 1999, when Brock and I were married at my dad's church in Shepherd, Texas. Many friends and family filled the sanctuary. Both mine and Brock's dad officiated the wedding which made it very special. Brian and Gin stood on the stage with us as well as a few others as Brock and I vowed to spend the rest of our lives together.

Everything was so perfect that day. It was just like the fairy tales I had read about in books. Brock and I were so in love. We had a ministry already in place that I was fitting into nicely. The future looked bright. I had no idea that catastrophe was just around the bend...

CHAPTER TWO
The Thief

"The thief comes only to steal and kill and destroy; I have come that they may have life, and have it to the full." John 10:10

I sat in the passenger seat of our Suburban reflecting on our friends' wedding we had just attended. "I cannot believe we just got married three months ago," I said looking over at Brock as he drove us home.

"We have done a lot in those three months," Brock said smiling.

"That's an understatement!" I commented as I thought back on the thirty youth camps we had participated in over the last few months.

We would perform each night of camp, and then, after everyone left the auditorium, we rehearsed our show for the next day. I was living off a few hours of sleep a night.

Brock saved up every penny he made from the shows he did over the last couple of years and bought sound equipment, lighting, and some custom-built stage props. The church he worked with in Texarkana bought him a twelve-foot trailer to haul the gear.

A couple of people traveled with us that summer to operate the sound and lighting. I assisted Brock onstage. Therefore, I spent most of our late night practices learning "The Puppet Master."

This was our focal piece using a grand illusion. A grand illusion was a big stage prop which enabled a girl to disappear or gave the impression someone was cut in half, or something of the sort. Since the illusion we owned cost $5,000, we only had one.

This particular effect began with a box onstage. The box had three-foot legs and big windows without panes on each side so that you could see it was completely empty.

Brock would then enter the scene dressed in all black with a half black, half white mask over his face. He stood up on the box and covered it with a cloth. Suddenly the cloth would rise on its own and a form would emerge. Brock would pull the cloth away to reveal me standing inside the box with my head down and eyes closed.

Then, Brock produced a marionette cross and held it over my head. He would move my arms and head on command. It looked as if I was a limp doll and he was my master. We had everything choreographed to the dramatic music.

I was led all over the stage doing things like smoking and drinking and worrying what I looked like in a mirror. In the end, I was sitting inside of the box with a needle in my arm. I mimicked shooting up drugs and then collapsed inside the box.

Brock would cover the box again. With a quick motion, he removed the cloth showing that I had disappeared.

After the act, Brock would tell the audience you will serve one master and he quoted a scripture from Romans chapter six. "Either you serve yourself, in which Satan ultimately has control, or you will serve God. It can only be one or the other." Brock would conclude with, "Who is your master?"

The first night I performed "The Puppet Master," I felt so alive! It was as if this was what I was created to do.

When I saw how many people responded to Jesus because of it, my heart soared. All of those sleepless nights were worth it.

I was pulled back to the present when I realized we were close to being home. "I wish I could sleep for a week! Do we have to move today?" I asked Brock, knowing the answer to my question.

We were moving into a new house across town. In between shows that summer, I boxed up all our belongings. Everything was ready to be moved into the new place.

"Chad and Rebecca are meeting us at the house to help us move tonight, plus I've already rented the moving truck," Brock looked over at me sympathetically. "Don't worry. Chad and I will get everything moved in and you can unpack the boxes next month if you want to."

"You know that I'm going to want to get unpacked as quickly as possible."

"I know. Just don't kill yourself trying to do it in one night! Our schedule is much lighter over the next few months. You will have time to relax."

My brow furrowed with worry as I asked. "Do you think we will have enough money to live off of? I mean with me quitting my job and working full time with you, we now only have one income and no roommates to split the mortgage. We are barely scraping by."

This was something I knew firsthand. Brock was good at many things, but balancing a checkbook was not one of them. I was slightly better than Brock, so we decided this would be my job.

"Did you see how effective the shows were this summer?" Brock asked.

I nodded.

"Tell me, is God using us to change people's lives?"

I nodded more enthusiastically this time.

"Then God will provide. We are right in the middle of His will. He called me to use my show to tell His gospel. He called you to be my helpmate. Nothing can stop us!"

My spirits lifted as we pulled into our driveway. Brock always knew what to say.

I looked over at him and noticed his face go white and fear was in his eyes. After a speech like that, why would he be scared?

"What?" I asked.

"Where is the trailer?"

My face grew hot and sweat beads began forming on my forehead. I whipped my head around to the spot where the trailer had been. It was not there anymore. Suddenly the world felt off kilter.

"No! No! No! There has to be an explanation!" I yelled jumping out of the Suburban and slamming the door.

Brock grabbed his cell phone and dialed 9-1-1 as he joined me in the location the trailer had once been.

"Yes, I'd like to report a theft."

Our engaged friends, Chad and Rebecca, drove up. "Plans have changed," Brock told them after hanging up the phone. "Our trailer with our whole show inside has been stolen!"

A police officer was at our house shortly and took a report.

Before the cop left, Brock asked him, "Honestly, what are the chances of ever finding my trailer?"

"Considering that there has been a ring of trailer thefts in Texas lately and we have not recovered any of the stolen trailers, not good. I'm sorry."

Brock and Chad walked the officer out to his car trying to get any information that would help us find our trailer.

I sat on the couch stunned. The officer's words rang in my head.

Rebecca sat down on the couch next to me and placed my hands in hers. I looked up at her pretty face.

In her sweet voice, Rebecca said, "Have you thanked God for your trailer being stolen yet?"

I gasped with surprise. I was in shock that our whole show was stolen from us. I was shocked that this was actually happening, but Rebecca's question sent me over the edge.

"I...uh...I...um, I need to use the restroom," I stood up and fled to the bathroom.

I locked the door and sunk down to the floor. My back rested against the wall of the tub and my legs were drawn up against my chest. I wrapped my arms around my knees and hot tears slid down my cheeks.

A few minutes later, I heard a couple of knocks and Rebecca say, "I didn't mean to upset you. I was trying to be encouraging."

I mustered up all the strength I had left after my cry and rose to my feet.

Opening the door, I said, "I know what you meant. God's always in control. I am just confused as to why He let this happen."

"I'm sorry," Rebecca said and hugged me.

****

A week later, I sat in our new town house amongst several boxes. I didn't have the will power to unpack. It had been the worst week of my life.

Brock had called our auto insurance company to inform them about the theft and see what they could do. We assumed the trailer itself would be covered since it was written in our policy, but were unsure if the equipment inside, worth $20,000, would be taken care of.

They gave us bad news. Not only would we not be reimbursed for the gear, but we would not receive a dime for the trailer either. There was some loophole in our policy. In order to be compensated for the trailer, it must have been hooked up to our truck at the time it was lifted.

A few nights after the theft, we went to see a movie to try and get our mind off the whole incident. We were in between banks since we were switching to one closer to our new house. Brock had every penny we had in his wallet that night...$250. After the movie, Brock realized his wallet had slipped out of his pocket. After searching for half an hour, we found the wallet, but the cash was missing.

For the first few days after the trailer went missing, Brock fought. After our cash was stolen, the fight left him. This man, who was usually the life of the party, spent days sitting on his bed staring at the wall. He didn't give any of his inspiring speeches or humorous jokes like he usually did when problems arose. He didn't say anything. He just gazed off into the distance, his eyes looking dead.

For the first time, I was angry with God. How could He call us to do this ministry, but then allow the means to do it to be stripped away? We literally had nothing! I had been a part of this ministry for three months. Was this it for me? Three months and then it's over?

In the past, I would run to the Lord the first moment something did not go according to plan. I realized that I had not really prayed about the theft. In fact, in my anger, I had skipped my daily times with the Lord.

"Lord, I can't handle this!" I yelled. The words seemed to bounce off the walls of my empty living room.

"Good," I heard the Lord say in my spirit. "Now maybe you will let Me take over."

"Lord, what should I do?" I said out loud my voice filled with defeat.

"PRAY SPECIFICALLY AND I WILL SHOW YOU MY POWER." The words were so close to audible that I glanced around the room to make sure I was alone.

I could not see anyone, but I could feel the presence of the Lord fill the room. Goosebumps appeared on my arms. A peace replaced the anxiety that had been building inside of me the last few days.

"Okay, I need $545 to pay the rent next week and $50 for food to get us through the end of this week. So right now, I'm asking you for $595 specifically," I said to the Lord.

I decided to wait and see what happened before I told Brock about the instruction I had just received from God.

The next day, Brock and I drove to Louisiana to speak at Brock's dad's church. His parents were out of town, so Brock would be taking his place this morning.

"Are they going to pay you for speaking?" I asked Brock as he drove.

"Yes, they will give us $150."

I thought, "That's a long way from $595."

"What are you going to speak about?" I asked Brock.

"I have an idea," he answered his mood still unusually melancholy.

I sat on the aisle in the second row as Brock began to speak. I had never seem him speak without using an illusion to demonstrate.

As he spoke, it was obvious he was broken. However, in his humble state, his words were touching. He seemed to have more passion and authority. By the end, I was moved to tears. I heard a few sniffles in the crowd and glanced behind me. Many others were touched as well.

After saying our goodbyes, we sat back in the Suburban to drive home. As Brock cranked the engine, he held up a $50 bill.

"Someone gave me this! We had enough gas in our tank to get us here, but I was praying specifically for $50 to get us home," he said with a smile.

"Oh, and here are some checks," Brock said handing me a small stack.

"There's more than one?" I asked.

"Everyone had heard about what happened and some wanted to help us out."

I quickly added up the checks.

"How much is it?" He questioned.

"Five hundred ninety-five dollars," I whispered as I dropped my hand in my lap. An excitement bubbled up from my soul. God had answered my prayer and Brock's to the penny!

"Brock, we have to pray specifically. You asked the Lord for $50, right? Well, I asked him yesterday for $595. Not $600, but $595, and that is what I am holding in my hand right now!"

Brock began to smile for the first time in a week. He pumped his fist in the air and said, "Yes! God is not done with this ministry yet!"

"I have a feeling this is only the beginning," I said feeling more hope than I had experienced before.

I immediately got a notebook from my bag, and wrote down all of the items we needed to replace what was in the trailer. It took three legal sized papers to list them, but somehow I knew the Lord would provide.

****

A few months after the theft, I stared out the window of our house eagerly waiting for our truck to return. We traded our Suburban for a used box truck. It looked like a U-Haul truck but was solid white and had a lift gate on the back so we could easily get our equipment in and out.

We found out that IBM in Dallas was getting rid of some used road cases for a fraction of the price of new ones. Our friend was heading to Dallas for business and offered to pick the cases up for us.

"He's here!" I exclaimed when I saw the truck pull in the driveway.

We both ran outside and Brock rolled up the back door of the truck to reveal five road cases. These cases were sturdy boxes with wheels on the bottom that could easily be rolled out of the truck and onto a stage. It was made to protect the gear inside of it.

The cases varied in size, the smallest being three feet wide and three feet tall and the largest being eight feet wide and four feet tall. We pulled each case onto the lawn and opened them to see inside.

"We paid $300 for all of these cases?" I asked.

"Yes! That's such a great deal! Normally, it would cost that much for the smallest one," Brock said excitedly.

"Why are they usually so pricey?"

"Because ordinarily you get your gear, like sound equipment, or whatever, and you measure it. Then, the company that builds these cases, builds them to the exact measurements you give them."

"Oh, so that the gear fits snugly in each case," I said, comprehending why they were so valuable. "So, we did it completely backwards, because we have road cases, but no equipment to put in them yet."

"I know," Brock said putting his arm around my shoulder. "But it was such a good deal that I could not pass it up."

Both of us scanned the front lawn with five empty cases and the empty truck. Brock sighed and said, "Now we need to pray the Lord will fill them up."

****

A few weeks later, we were headed to a friend's wedding in Shreveport, Louisiana. On the way, we went to Guitar Center to buy a new sound system. A couple we knew had given us the exact amount of money to buy JBL speakers just like the ones we had before.

Inside the store, I walked straight up to the JBL's. Brock was fixated on the Mackie speakers beside them.

"I heard these Mackie speakers are the best!" he said with longing.

"Brock, they are $200 more than the JBL's, and we don't have an extra $200. Let's just get the ones we came to get."

"What if the Lord wants us to get the better speakers?"

"Then He would have provided us with $1,800 instead of the $1,600 I have in my pocket," I answered. "Now are you ready to get them and go to the wedding?"

"No, I'll make you a deal. Let's pray for the extra $200. If the Lord provides it, we get the Mackies. If not, we'll come back and purchase the JBL's."

"Deal," I said.

I saw Rebecca at the reception and quickly ran to sit next to her. "Hey girl!"

"Hey!" she said giving me a quick side hug. "Before I forget, see that girl in the purple dress over there?"

I looked over and saw a girl who I didn't recognize.

"She goes to my church and heard about your trailer being stolen. She said that the Lord told her to give you this." Rebecca then handed me an envelope.

When I opened it, my heart did a flip. The only thing inside was $200 in cash.

"Rebecca, we were just praying for $200 specifically," I said as tears began to surface.

"Awww. Isn't the Lord good?" She said.

"Yes, He is. In fact, I think that I am ready to thank Him for the trailer being stolen now. He is showing me His power and provision in ways I have never experienced. That would not have been possible had it not been for the trailer being stolen."

That night, we put our new Mackie speakers in one of the road cases. It fit to the quarter inch! It was as if the case was made for it. To add to the miracle, the original speakers we planned to purchase were much bigger than the ones we ended up getting and would have been too big for the case.

Over the next several months, word spread about our theft. One of our friends wrote a newsletter for us explaining our loss and how we needed support.

The church my dad pastored took up an offering for us. At a youth event we performed at, the guest speaker led the audience in taking up a collection to go toward purchasing new gear.

Rick Rowe, a newscaster from Shreveport, Louisiana who periodically covered religious events, came to our house and interviewed Brock about our catastrophes of recent months. It aired on television broadcasting over west Louisiana and east Texas.

Not only did money begin to pour in, but we had more prayer coverage than we could have asked for. We felt backed and not alone.

Through all of this, a Christian booking agency found us. They took over the administrative part of our ministry that we could not do from the road. This agency provided more opportunities to perform.

Six months after the trailer was stolen, I checked my last item off the specific prayer request list. The Lord answered every request down to the smallest detail. I was so grateful in how faithful God had been. However, future circumstances would quickly change my thankful attitude.

CHAPTER THREE
The Bubble Car

"You have not because you ask not." James 4:2

It was July of the following year, and I tried not to be ungrateful as I drove our box truck to the bank. It was comforting not to have a trailer to worry about getting stolen. However, since the truck was our only vehicle, we had to use it to drive around town as well.

Earlier that year, we moved to a town in the Houston area. We had clicked with one of the youth pastors, Todd, in the city at an event we had participated in. He then asked us to go on their youth ski trip. We bonded so much with the youth group that we decided to move to their town.

Todd had been a good friend to us. He immediately plugged us into the youth group when we were home and showed us around town.

"It's much more expensive to live here than where we lived before," I thought as I looked around at the new shopping centers I was passing.

Paying the rent and monthly note for the truck was draining our bank account. Since we had a new booking agency supporting us, we were booking more shows, but they were not consistent.

I wished we had several shows a month. When we performed, I felt alive and empowered! Doing things like running errands at home seemed so dull in comparison.

My mind drifted back to our last show the preceding week at a church in a small Texas town.

We could not afford to take anyone to the shows to run sound and lighting. Therefore, I had to find a way to manage all of it. I trained volunteers provided by the local host to run the lights. We set up a black curtain onstage. I stationed myself behind the curtain and pushed "play" on our music player and controlled the volume on the sound board. When needed, I ran onstage to take Brock a prop or participate in an illusion.

I also took on the role of producing the show. Brock discovered my background in the study of psychology aided me in knowing what trick brings out what emotion and when in the show that particular effect needed to go. I began to arrange the show in a formula. The first presentation was impressive set to music followed by a comedic trick using a volunteer from the audience. The third act was some sort of escape or stunt that brought tension. This was followed by comedy relief. Then, we would perform the illusion that segued into the message about Jesus.

Being assistant, stage manager, and production manager kept me running all night.

After we performed "The Puppet Master," I lay down on the floor backstage and listened as Brock began to speak about the saving grace of Jesus. It was the first time I could catch my breath. I wiped the sweat from my brow and tried to slow my beating heart.

I began to pray as I normally did, "Lord, this is Your part of the show. You come and invade people's lives tonight. Only You can touch their souls."

That's when it happened. A stillness came over the room. A presence so powerful and mighty entered the auditorium and hung in the air. Goosebumps formed on my skin. I sat up and looked around almost expecting to see Jesus standing there. I froze in awe of this spectacular Spirit.

A few moments later, I breathed, reminding myself where I was. I needed to continue praying for the ones in attendance. Then, I felt the Holy Spirit say, "I am already working on the people here, but I want to focus on you."

At that time, I forgot everything around me except the presence of the Lord. The amount of love and acceptance exuding from the Holy Spirit was more than I could handle. Emotion overtook me as I realized how unworthy I was to be in the company of God. I sat up on my knees and dropped my head to the floor as I began to repent. I experienced sweet release as I felt the forgiveness of God as I had many times before.

Just then, Brock called all of the ones who were being drawn to the Lord for the first time to stand up. I peaked out the curtain and saw many people all over the crowd pop up. Tears began to flow as understanding set in that the Lord was working in individual people's lives all over the room. He could talk so intimately with me as well as the other couple hundred in attendance at the same time.

The memory faded as I pulled into the parking lot of the bank. Only then did I remember that this particular location did not have a lobby, only a drive-thru. The drive-thru was eleven feet tall. Our truck was thirteen and a half feet. I had to make a choice: drive all the way across town to another bank or suffer the humiliation of walking through the drive-thru. I swallowed my pride and did the latter.

I walked up to the lane farthest from the window hoping the car next to me would shield the fact that I had no car. As soon as I reached the column, the car pulled away leaving me completely exposed. Immediately, I heard a voice welcoming me on the intercom. Midway through her hello, the teller looked up and saw me standing there. We were now looking eye to eye. A laugh escaped her lips before she could get all of the words out.

I explained to her about not clearing the roof of the drive-thru. She glanced over in the direction I was pointing and spotted my truck.

"That's awfully big for you to be driving," she said, her laugh turning into a sympathetic smile.

A short time into the transaction, I realized that I left something in the truck. I had to tell the lady to wait as I went to retrieve the missing article. Frustration began to build as I thought about how inconvenient this truck was for running errands.

When I got home, I slammed the front door.

"What's wrong?" Brock asked.

"I had to walk through the drive-thru at the bank," I said feeling sorry for myself.

Brock chuckled as he asked, "Did the bank lady think it was funny?"

"Yes, but I didn't!" I looked at him.

"I've got something that will cheer you up," Brock said holding out a check for $1,000.

"From our taxes?"

He nodded.

"I wish we could get a car. It would make my life at home so much easier," I mumbled.

"What if we can!" he said looking hopeful. "What if we can find a car for $1,000?"

"If we can find a car for that price today, we'll buy it!" I said feeling more optimistic.

I bought a newspaper and scoured the car ads while Brock drove us to the used car lots in town.

My hope quickly diminished. Nothing in the paper fit our price range, and so far the cheapest car we found on a lot was $3,000. It did not even run.

After a few hours, we gave up and began heading home. I could not hide my disappointment. I can only imagine how downcast I appeared when Brock said, "I found it!" He pulled into another used car lot.

There, sitting right beside the road was the most hideous car I had ever seen. Everything was spray painted silver excluding the windows. Even the wheels, tires, and bumpers were silver. Clear, Christmas ball ornaments were siliconed to every surface of the car.

Brock said, "See the price on the window, $995?" He jumped out of our truck and began talking with a salesman.

I was in shock at the sight. After a few minutes, I walked over to meet up with Brock.

"Does it run well?" I heard Brock ask.

The man answered, "It runs great and only has sixty thousand miles on it."

"It looks like a third grader decorated it," I said interrupting their conversation.

"Close," the salesclerk said. "A fourth grade class did it. Each student put something inside the balls and the teacher attached them to the car. It was in the art car parade in Houston a few weeks ago."

"What kind of car is it?" Brock asked. You could not see the name or really even the body style due to the spray paint and balls.

"Let me check our records," the man said as he walked toward his office.

When he was out of sight, Brock looked to me and said, "What do you think?"

I began to grin and said, "I actually like it! If you are going to buy a clunker, it may as well have personality."

"It definitely has personality," Brock chuckled.

Just then, the salesman returned with paperwork in hand. "This car is a Celebrity."

"That's very fitting," I commented.

"We will take it!" Brock said.

I drove the truck home while Brock drove our "new" car home. We both stopped to get fuel.

When we were inside the gas station, Brock said, "I've been getting strange looks ever since we left the lot. One lady was so distracted that she ran into the guard rail!"

"Oh no! Is she okay?"

"Yes, she wasn't going very fast, but I need to get those balls cleaned off of it before we cause any more accidents."

"Look!" I said pointing outside to where our car was parked. A couple of girls were standing next to it while a guy was taking a picture of them and the car.

"Our car is a celebrity!" Brock said laughing.

****

A few months later, Todd invited us to attend a small Bible study group from church. It took place at a couple's house in a new subdivision in town.

"Wow!" I told Brock as we drove up to a two-story brick home. "This is a nice house! These people are our age and own this house?"

At that moment, I was very self conscious about our car. Brock had removed the balls, but the silicone would not come off. Now it had thick, raised white polka dots all over it.

"I think I'll park two houses down," Brock said as he passed by the house.

Todd introduced us to everyone when we entered. We began talking with a few people in the kitchen.

I then heard some commotion in the living room beside the front door. "Come here!" The owner of the house said motioning toward the front window. "You have to see the car at the neighbor's house! It's hideous!"

I looked over the direction he pointed and saw several people peering out the window. "What is that thing?" someone said.

Many began to snicker. "I hope they don't keep it parked there for long. It's definitely an eye sore," said another guy, patting the homeowner on the back.

Brock and I froze as the people we were talking with ran to catch the grotesque sight.

I looked to see if Todd was within earshot. He knew the car belonged to us. He must have been in another room, because I did not spot him.

"Don't say anything," Brock said.

"Good call," I agreed.

We left early that night so nobody would know that we were the owners of the appalling car.

"You were quiet on the drive home," Brock said as we walked up the sidewalk to our townhouse.

I plopped down on one of the two steps before we reached our front door. I was not ready to go inside.

Looking up at the stars, I said, "I think we should stick with hanging out with the youth. That was mortifying!"

Brock sat down putting his arm around me. "Do you wish we had a house and nice car?"

"Actually, no," I paused. "When we are on the road, it feels natural. I know exactly what to do and when to do it. It's the home life I don't have figured out."

"What if we could take our home on the road?" Brock asked.

"How?"

He explained that he had been looking into semi-trucks with RV conversions. Behind the driver's and passenger's seat was a bed, couch, table with benches, kitchenette with stove top and refrigerator, and a bathroom. They were called totorhomes. The diesel engines were known to last up to a million miles.

"We could pull a trailer with our show equipment in it. We could even put a car in the trailer," he said with excitement.

"How did you even hear about these totorhomes? At the Christian events we have gone to, I've only seen tour buses or vans."

"The race car community uses these and I stumbled across one on the internet. It would function like a tour bus, but it's a tenth of the cost."

"I bet they are still very expensive. How can we afford it?"

"If we combine what we pay for rent and our truck, it would cover the note. Plus, we would save money, because we wouldn't need to stay in hotels."

"So you want us to live on the road all the time? Not have a house or apartment or anything?"

Untypical for Brock, he sounded unsure when he said, "That's what I'm saying, yes."

I looked back up at the dark sky and thought about what he was suggesting. There was a whole world out there I wanted to explore. Not having to come back home after every show would make it easier to go new places.

I thought back to when I went on vacation with my family as a child. Every time we drove into a state I had not been to before, I pleaded with my dad to stop at the welcome center. There I collected brochures about the state. I learned the state birds and capitals. I read about what kinds of food they were famous for. I made a goal then to someday travel to all 50 states. Maybe living on the road full time would enable me to achieve this childhood dream.

"What do you think?" Brock asked, breaking into my thoughts.

"I think it could work," I said.

Brock leaped up from the step. "So you are on board?"

I stood up and jumped to the step above Brock making my 5'2" body match up better to Brock's 6'4" frame. Then, I put my hands on his shoulders.

"It sounds like an adventure! Just one thing, though," I said thoughtfully. "We have to sell our box truck."

The truck had been anything but reliable. Several days we were stranded at a repair shop in between the place where we were performing and home. When it rained it leaked right on our heads. The drip, drip, drip was torturous.

"I'll put a 'For Sale' sign on it, but you are right. It will be a tough sale," Brock said shaking his head.

"Sometimes I wish that truck would just blow up!" I said frustrated just thinking about all the problems it accrued.

A few months later, my wish came true.

CHAPTER FOUR
Hot Winter Night

"His work will be shown for what it is, because the Day will bring it to light. It will be revealed with fire, and the fire will test the quality of each man's work." I Corinthians 3:13

I shot out of the bed with a start! I tried to remember where we were as my eyes began adjusting to the darkness. The living room and kitchen came into focus and the memory of Brock's birthday party the night before came floating back to mind. We were at our friend's apartment in Birmingham, Alabama. After doing a few shows in the area, we decided to stay a couple of extra days and hang out with friends.

Why did I wake up so abruptly? It wasn't the uncomfortable sofa bed. I can sleep anywhere. "The gift of the road," we called it. No, something else woke me.

I could hear Brock pick up his cell phone and say a tired "hello."

That's what it was! The phone was ringing. What time was it? It felt like I had just gone to sleep. Glancing at the clock on the shelf next to me told me it was 5:02 a.m.

"Yes, sir. I'll be right there." Brock said and then hung up the phone. He calmly began to put on his pants and shoes.

"Well!" I said jumping to my feet. "What's going on?"

"That was the police. They got my number off the 'For Sale' sign on our truck," he said as he began tying his shoe laces.

"The police calling you in the middle of the night is not good," I interjected. "What's wrong?"

"Our truck is on fire," Brock said nonchalantly.

I felt my stomach drop. I mentally began scanning the inventory of our truck. All of the things we had acquired after the theft. Were they all gone? Only a year and a half after the trailer theft, would we lose it all again?

I began peppering him with questions as I threw on my shoes and clothes. "How? Is it all burned? What about our show stuff?"

"The officer didn't tell me any specifics," he said as he walked out the door to the parking lot.

I quickly put on my jacket and ran after him.

The cool air hit me as I walked outside on this January morning. However, I didn't notice the temperature as I followed Brock out into the spacious lot. All I could think about was our equipment.

As we walked past a set of garages, I could see smoke billowing up from where our truck sat. I ran to the back of the truck where our gear was.

A fireman had bolt cutters in his hand. With one quick motion, he snapped the padlock on the back of the truck and lifted the garage door.

Thick, black smoke poured out of the back. I closed my eyes and began to cough as smoke filled my throat.

After a few seconds, I opened one eye to try and get a glimpse into the box part of the truck.

"It looks like everything made it back here. Good thing you have these cases," the fireman said patting one of the road cases we got from IBM with his gloved hand. "They took the brunt of the smoke."

I sighed with relief. Soot was caked onto the cases. The once blue color had turned to solid black, but other than some smoke damage, they were fine. The road cases did their job. They protected the illusions, sound equipment, and lighting inside.

"Unfortunately," the fireman said in a thick, southern accent, "the truck is toast."

Brock and I followed him to the front of the truck. I gasped as I saw the front bumper and whole engine of the truck melted down to a

3" chunk of metal. The front seats were charred with pieces of the leather continuously flaking off and flying into the air. Ashes filled the small area behind the driver's seat.

"How did you guys hear about the fire?" Brock asked.

The police officer stepped in and said a person leaving their apartment that morning came outside to see a blazing fire and called 9-1-1.

"What do you think caused this?" I asked the fireman.

"Well, it looks like it started in the engine. Flames were burning the wall separating your cab from the box when we got here," he answered.

"I did just get some electrical work done in the engine," Brock said looking confused.

"When was that?" asked the officer.

"Three days ago," Brock said not taking his eyes off our cauterized truck.

"That's probably it," said the man with the accent.

After the police and fire department left, Brock and I stood speechless for several minutes.

"Oh no!" I said just realizing that it was the morning after Brock's birthday. "Your birthday gifts were destroyed." After the party at a local Mexican restaurant the night before, I had put the gifts Brock had received in the cab.

Brock sighed. "Well, at least our show gear was saved. That's all that matters."

I went to Brock and put my arm around his waist. "I guess we are going to get that totorhome after all," I said with a smile.

A strange feeling swirled inside of me. I knew I should be devastated that our truck blew up, but I was not. It reminded me of a day in high school when we were standing on the football field due to a bomb threat. A girl next to me was anxious, worried it was real. The guy next to her was relieved because he was missing a test he was not prepared for. I had an exhilaration pumping through me just because it was unusual. It was not a typical, boring day. This day was an adventure!

****

I plopped down in a chair by our merchandise table where we sold t-shirts and "Brock Gill" stickers and such. I realized it had been eight hours since I had sat down last.

This day had been a typical show day. Eight men from the church helped me load in everything and set up our black curtains and sound system. Then, Brock and I set up all of the illusions backstage. After we checked the sound and lighting, I went to the lobby and set up our product table. This took four hours. The show was an hour and a half. Then, it took another two hours to tear down all of our gear and put them back in the cases and eventually back into the truck.

Our truck had burned January 7 and it had been three weeks since then. In those few weeks, we had done fifteen shows using a Penske rental truck to get us and our gear to and from each show. The rental was a great deal, but we had to turn it in every three days in order to get the best value. This meant we had to unload and load the truck again every few days. Sometimes, Brock and I had to do it by ourselves. Transporting seven large road cases and a few boxes, along with half a dozen large suitcases every three days on top of our regular show day, was exhausting.

It was now 10:30 p.m. and I had everything loaded except the product table.

I threw my head back and sighed, "Of course our truck had to blow up on the busiest month we have ever had," I thought. This month we had 21 shows, three times the amount we normally did.

The elderly lady who had volunteered to run our table that night came up to me in the chair and patted my leg. "If you need to take a smoke break, there is a private spot around the back."

"What?" I asked.

"It's okay. My sister has been trying to quit for years. It's hard to do."

"Oh," I said with a chuckle. "I don't smoke. Our stuff just smells like smoke because our truck caught on fire a few weeks ago."

"A few weeks ago?" The lady said with surprise. "It smells like it happened a few hours ago."

"I know," I said with frustration. "I have Febreezed everything numerous times, but it's still pretty bad. Believe it or not, the stench is better than it was."

"Bless your heart," the lady replied sympathetically.

A few guys helped load up the rest of the gear into the rental truck. One of the men handed Brock a check for $1,000 at the end.

"This is to go toward your new truck," he said.

We thanked him and drove a few towns over to Dallas where we had to be up early in the morning to perform at a school assembly.

The next day, we met the youth pastor in the lobby of the hotel. "Ready to get started?" he asked.

"Of course!" I answered sounding more energetic than I felt.

Brock and the pastor began discussing how Brock would do a smaller show at the school than the show he did at his church. He would do a few illusions and then give a message about making the right choices. Then, he would invite them to see the bigger show the following night where he would have the liberty to talk about Jesus.

As we walked out to the parking lot, Brock said, "School assemblies have been very effective for us so far. It builds a good relationship between the church and the school since they must have a certain number of assemblies a year, and your church is providing this for free. Also, it's great publicity to get people in the doors of your church who would not normally come..." His voice trailed off, and he stopped staring at the Penske truck we had rented.

I followed his eyes and saw what had him so stunned. The window on the passenger's side door was broken out. Glass fragments were all over the ground.

"No, no, no!" I yelled. "Not again!"

I followed Brock inside the truck to inspect what was missing. The youth pastor immediately picked up his cell phone and called the school where we were supposed to perform in an hour.

The burglar had gone into the back and opened every case. He took most of our merchandise.

"Your tackle box is missing," I said angrily. The only gift that survived the fire was Brock's new fishing tackle box. Now, it was lost as well.

The youth pastor arranged for the assembly to be moved to the afternoon, and Brock and I continued to go through every box.

We calculated about $3,000 worth of merchandise, magic props, and personal items were stolen.

Tears began to form in the corners of my eyes. I sat down on one of the cases and buried my face in my hands.

Brock sat down next to me, and I put my head on his chest softly crying.

"Can you imagine the disappointment the thief must have felt?" He said with a chuckle.

"This is a moving truck. He probably expected some furniture and a couple of TV's. I'm sure he was surprised to find magic props and sound gear instead."

I looked up at Brock's grin and a giggle escaped my lips. Delirium set in, and we began laughing uncontrollably.

After our laughter subsided, Brock kissed my head and said reassuringly, "We will get through this."

"I know. You and I can do anything together," I said repeating Brock's words from the night we began a romantic relationship. I leaned into his arms, drawing strength from his support.

****

The shows in Dallas went well despite the drama with the rental truck. We drove home eager to rest.

On the drive, I looked over at Brock and said, "This has been the most tiring month on the road. How did we make it through it?"

"I tell you what gets me through it. When I see how many people respond to the gospel of Jesus, I feel renewed, and all of the hard work is worth it," Brock answered.

"Whenever you give the gospel, I am backstage praying. The presence of the Lord is so thick in the room that I begin to get emotional. I've heard you speak over a hundred times, and I still fall to my knees weeping.

"I could do without this rental truck, though," I said changing the subject.

"We need $3,000 as a down payment in order to get the totorhome," Brock informed me.

"How much do we have now?"

"A couple of people in Dallas gave us $800 total."

I added it to the $1,000 the man had given us earlier. "So we need another $1,200," I said.

Brock's phone rang. As he answered it, I began to pray for the money we needed to purchase the new truck.

"That was Todd. He wants us to stop by his house on the way

home," Brock said.

Some of the youth group and leaders were gathered at Todd's house when we got there. They had heard about our struggles that month. After giving us some encouraging words, Todd handed us an envelope.

"We collected some money for you to go toward a new truck."

Brock peeked inside the envelope and added up the cash. "It's $1,200!" he said as he pumped the money into the air.

"That's what we were just praying for!" I exclaimed.

****

"I've got good news!" Brock said coming into the living room of our townhouse.

I looked up from the fiction book I was reading and smiled with anticipation.

"We have been booked for a student conference tour called 'Believe' for this fall and spring!" Brock continued. "The conference will go from Friday through Sunday afternoon every weekend. We will be performing and speaking each session."

"What cities are the conferences in?"

"All over the midwest, and also Portland and Los Angeles."

Excitement began to bubble up inside of me! Not only would we have some financial stability by having guaranteed shows the following year, but we would get to travel beyond Texas and the surrounding states where we usually performed.

"It's great timing to get the totorhome. When can we pick it up?" I asked.

Brock had already found the truck he wanted and had begun the paperwork. This totorhome had a Freightliner chassis with fourteen feet of living space built by United Specialties.

"Well, I am waiting to find out where we need to go to pick it up. The dealer's from Massachusetts but the manufacturer is in Indiana."

At that moment the phone rang. As Brock went to answer it, my mind filled with all the possibilities for adventures we could have on the tour and in our new totorhome.

"That was the dealer about our truck," Brock said breaking into my thoughts a few minutes later. "A couple who races is having a new totorhome built. In the meantime, this company has been letting them borrow the truck we are buying for the last month. So, next week we will go pick up our truck from their house."

"Where do they live?" I asked ready to form a plan on how to find the money to fly or drive to wherever they are to get the truck.

He grinned from ear to ear and said, "Pasadena, Texas—about an hour from here!"

Gratefulness filled my heart as I realized the implications. Out of all the trucks in the country, the Lord led us to one that was 45 miles away from our house.

****

In February of 2001, we boxed up our possessions and stored most of it in my parents' garage. We gave our bubble car to a youth pastor who was recently married and didn't have the funds to purchase a second vehicle. We bought a used, red Volkswagen Beetle. It fit nicely in the back of the 36' trailer we had acquired.

I looked around our new 14' home. Brock was getting our last stack of mail at the townhouse while I was decorating the living space of our truck that was sitting in the parking lot just outside.

The bed was over the cab of the truck. I chose a blue blanket to go on it, since the interior walls of the truck were grey and the couch and benches were blue with grey flecks. A couple of multicolor throw pillows added some pigmentation to the area. I attached pictures to the wall and had blue, red, and gold placemats on the table.

After emptying the last box, I sat down on the couch. My mom's words to me when we moved into our new house in Texas when I was sixteen years old came back to me. "Just think about all the memories we are about to make here," she said.

The back door opened and Brock came in handing me the last of our mail. In the future, we would have our mail sent to Brock's parents' house.

I began to flip through it when my eyes stopped on an envelope from our car insurance. It had finally come in. My hands shook as I opened the letter. Our insurance company had informed us that since it was a fire, we didn't have to pay our deductible, but we were not positive on how much they would give us for the old truck.

Brock noticed me opening the envelope. "How much?"

I answered, "$3,472."

"That's more than I expected," he said with a smile. "We are going to need that for the taxes on this truck."

"Do you think it will be that much?"

"Well, you know how taxes are hundreds of dollars when you buy a car?"

I nodded remembering paying some taxes on our Volkswagen a few weeks earlier.

"Our totorhome will cost thousands. I'm not sure how many thousands."

Later that week, we went to the Department of Motor Vehicles to pay the taxes. Both of us stood at the window waiting nervously for the lady behind the desk to tell us how much we had to pay.

"Oooh," she said pushing her glasses up higher on her nose as she looked at the computer screen. "You owe a lot of money," she said lowering her voice.

She then began scribbling something on a scrap of paper. With a sympathetic look, she slid the paper across the counter to us.

I looked down and read, "You owe $3,470."

I threw my head up as comprehension set in. God had done it again!

On our way out of the DMV, I asked Brock, "What should we do with our extra two dollars?"

He laughed. As we climbed up in our truck, he said, "I have been praying one prayer over and over recently. It's for power, protection, and provision. That was just one more example of His provision."

I thought about how the Lord had so miraculously shown provision in our lives. At our performances, when I saw how many lives were changed, I could clearly see His power.

I had no clue God's protection over us would become very evident in the coming months.

CHAPTER FIVE
Life on the Road

"Foxes have holes and birds of the air have nests, but the Son of Man has no place to lay His head." Matthew 8:20

My head was pounding with adrenaline as Brock and I opened the back door of our new truck and sat down on the sofa. We had just completed our first weekend at "Believe" youth conference. Not only had it been so exhilarating to perform, but also we really clicked with the people we worked with. That's why we were the last ones to leave the convention center. We enjoyed every minute of it. Plus, we did not have anywhere we had to be until the following weekend.

I pulled out the road atlas and asked Brock where he wanted to go that day. We had a week to get from our current location in Springfield, Missouri to Atlanta, Georgia.

"We could always go to Fort Pickens," Brock said with a smile.

Fort Pickens was a national park at the end of the peninsula in Pensacola Beach, Florida. We had camped in a tent there a couple of times before. This time, we had an RV to stay in.

"Sounds incredible," I said envisioning the sugar white sand and the emerald colored water.

We began the 735 mile journey. At 10 p.m. that night, Brock drove into a Flying J truck stop. After fueling up and dumping our septic tanks, he backed our 64' truck and trailer into a parking space in between two semi-trucks. We crawled up into our bed over the cab and went to sleep.

Early the next morning, I hopped down from the bed and got ready to take a shower. "Ugh!" I thought when I realized I didn't have any clean clothes in the truck and would have to go retrieve some out of the trailer.

I threw on a jacket over my pajamas and slipped on some sandals. When I opened the back door, light pierced my eyes. I blinked a few times before they came into focus.

As I opened the side door of the trailer, I had an eerie feeling I was being watched. I looked up at the side mirror of the truck parked next to us. The driver was looking into his mirror at me.

He looked away nervously and I quickly grabbed the closest suitcase and slammed the door. I hurried back in the truck and locked the back door.

"What is it?" Brock asked wearily sitting up slightly in bed.

"I had a weird feeling about the driver next to us."

"Wait for me before you go outside again," he answered.

After we both took quick showers in the truck, we decided to eat breakfast at the restaurant in the truck stop. I noticed on the way that the truck with the suspicious driver was gone.

"Look," Brock said pointing to some broken glass in the vacant parking spot next to us.

"Something fishy happened here this morning," I commented.

When we walked inside the gas station, a middle-aged couple was frantically talking to a police officer near the entrance.

"We were parked about halfway back along the wall next to the interstate," the man said to the cop.

"That's where we were parked," Brock said approaching the couple. "What happened?"

The lady dabbed her tears with a tissue and said, "Our truck was stolen while we were eating breakfast."

We figured out that their truck was parked two spots away from us. The semi that was parked next to us was covering while his partner lifted the truck.

"I saw one of the thieves," I said as realization sunk in. Suddenly I lost my appetite.

After the officer wrote down my eye witness account, we skipped breakfast and hit the road.

****

I breathed in the salty air. After two relaxing days on the beach, the creepy look on the truck thief's face had faded from memory.

I looked over at Brock sitting in a lawn chair next to me and smiled. "This is the life."

"I agree," he answered settling deeper into his chair.

I looked around the barren beach. All of the families that had spent the day here had gone home or to their hotels. The clouds took on a pinkish hue as the sun began its descent.

A young man and woman walked by hand in hand. The short, stocky guy took off his shoes and darted into the water soaking his jeans and t-shirt. The thin girl giggled as she followed his lead.

We watched curiously as they bounded through the first few waves. Both of them stood about 25 yards out jumping in and out of the waves.

A few minutes later, I noticed a man approaching. He stopped in front of us and looked out at the swimmers. Then, he glanced at us strangely. He shrugged and continued to walk by.

I looked back to the water and saw the man that was swimming waving his hands. The pounding surf drowned out his voice but I could read his lips. "Help!" He was yelling.

The top of the girl's head bobbed to the surface.

"Brock!" I exclaimed patting him on the arm. "They need help!"

Immediately, Brock jumped up taking his phone out of his pocket and handing it to me. He ran into the ocean after the couple.

I wondered what could be wrong. The guy could obviously touch the bottom. They were not too far out. Maybe they were drunk. I had heard stories of people drowning when they were inebriated.

I stood to my feet as I saw Brock pick the girl up in his arms. The man held onto Brock's arm as well.

After a slight struggle, Brock let both of them go and turned toward me. "Go get help!" He yelled pointing behind me.

Panic began to rise up. Was Brock in trouble? Was he drowning? The waves looked slightly more turbulent than normal but not anything Brock could not handle. His tall frame could manage four feet of water. Plus, he was an excellent swimmer. He would be able to push through the waves when they surged above his head.

Frantically, I ran down the beach a few yards and up the first set of stairs in sight. All the way, I was screaming for help.

When I reached the top of the stairs I ascended onto a pool deck. A circular bar surrounded by men with drinks in their hands was a few feet to the left.

I ran up to it yelling hysterically. "Two people are drowning and my husband went out to save them. Now he is drowning too!"

One chubby man said an expletive and took off his watch laying it on the bar. He and a few other men stood from their bar stools and began to walk toward me. The bartender lady picked up the phone.

They slowly approached me. I took off sprinting back toward the ocean. What if Brock was dying? I flew back down the steps taking them two at a time. When my feet hit the sand, I saw Brock and the couple in knee-deep water walking to the shore.

I breathed in a sigh of relief. My heart began to beat less wildly. The two men who made it down the steps with me turned back informing the ones following that everyone was okay.

Brock, the girl, and the guy all separately fell down to the sand breathing hard. The guy sat up and said, "Thank you man! If you had not come out, we would have drowned. We have both grown up in

Florida and have never experienced anything like that before."

"Let's go back home to Tallahassee. I don't want to be here anymore," the woman mumbled to her boyfriend.

After one more quick thanks, they both left the beach.

I sat down beside Brock where he was still lying on the ground. "What happened?" I asked confused.

He explained that when he went out to the couple, the girl was already bobbing up and down. When he picked her up, the fight left her and she went limp. Then, the guy grabbed a hold of his arm as he was struggling as well.

Brock was bewildered as to why they would be drowning when the water was not over their heads until he turned around and tried to take his first step toward shore. A wall of water up to his chest was forcefully pushing against him out to sea. After Brock told me to go get help, he planted his feet one at a time until he made it back to shallow water. A couple of times, the people panicked and began to swing their arms, almost drowning Brock, so he had to let them go for a few seconds while he gained a sturdy stance.

Pride for my husband began to fill my heart. He wasn't like the guy who walked by and did nothing. Brock was a man of action.

"Whew!" I said. "This life on the road is crazy! A few days ago, I witnessed a semi being stolen and today you save two adults from drowning in the ocean!"

"It's definitely been exciting," Brock said as he started walking back to where we parked.

"I have to go to bed now," he said wearily.

"But it's only 8:30."

"That wore me out!"

****

A couple of months later, I stretched out on the couch in our truck which was parked a few blocks from the convention center where the conference was being held. It was Saturday afternoon, the only time we got to rest all weekend. The late nights and early mornings it took to do this tour were wearing on me.

Brock opted to get coffee down the street with a friend who lived locally. I had the 14' living quarters all to myself.

Flipping through the channels on our twenty inch television, I settled on a *Law & Order* rerun. Shortly into the episode, I drifted off to sleep.

I awoke to a knock on the back door. I began to stumble toward it, assuming it was Brock. Strangers always approached the door up by the driver's seat and not the back door. Since there were no windows at the back, I glanced out the side window to see if I could see anyone on the street. Standing on the sidewalk on the other side of the road was the friend Brock was just with. This affirmed my assumption.

"We really need to get two sets of keys," I mumbled, aggravated I was woken from my sleep.

As I put my hand on the door to unlock it, a scripture darted its way into my thoughts. "Don't be afraid. For I am with you."

I jerked my arm back from the door. Why did that verse come to mind at this moment?

Moving a few feet away, I called Brock on my cell phone.

"Hi," he answered. "I am about to leave the coffee shop."

"You are not at the back door right now?" I asked with a slight tremor. I frantically filled him in. He told me to sit tight and not open the door until he got there.

I looked out the window again and did not see the guy anymore. It must have been a man that looked like our friend.

I pulled down the shades on all the windows, turned off the

television, and curled up on the couch. What did the Lord just save me from?

Tears began to fall as I imagined all of the horrible scenarios. "Lord, I am so glad You have my back. Living on the road can be dangerous."

****

I found that it was difficult to get Brock's mind off of work. He commented about the lighting in a restaurant or the music playing in the gas station. Could we somehow take what they were playing or displaying and adapt it to our show?

I, on the other hand, needed a break. The adventure of literally living on the road was exhilarating, but not having a set place to come home to was tiring.

When he suggested we begin riding dirt bikes, I jumped on it thinking this could be an activity that had nothing to do with work. That Christmas, we purchased two dirt bikes. A large one to fit Brock's height and a small one to fit me.

We bought the bikes in Brock's parents' small Louisiana town. He immediately began riding his bike around the yard and throughout his parents' neighborhood. It thrilled me to see how excited he was to be back on a bike again after getting rid of his as a teenager.

A few minutes later, I walked inside his parent's house. I heard his dad talking on the phone. "I'm going to have to call you back," he was saying. "My son is driving his bike through the yard with a bag over his head!"

I ran into the office where his dad had just hung up the phone and peered through the window. There was Brock doing crazy eights with a black bag over his head.

"I'll go check it out," I said not too surprised. This wasn't the first time I saw Brock doing something bizarre.

I ran outside and yelled over the engine for Brock to stop! He came barreling toward me. Right before I jumped to the side, he came to an abrupt stop.

He took off the bag and covering his eyes was a black blindfold. He then took the blindfold off. "What are you doing?" I asked with a slight chuckle.

"I've seen magicians drive cars on the street blindfolded, but I've never seen anyone do it on a dirt bike. Plus, I can ride a dirt bike inside," he answered confidently.

"That's actually a great idea. Just riding a dirt bike inside is exciting, but adding a blindfold takes it up a notch," I said picturing the effect. "So, I guess you have found a way to use this for work."

He quickly sat the bike on the kickstand and brought his arms around my waist.

"We will only use it for work on occasion. Whenever I ride for fun, I won't be thinking about this effect or any work at all."

"You promise?" I asked feeling it was important for him to have a hobby. I read fiction books and watched action films. Brock needed a way to escape, too. Otherwise, I felt burnout would eventually overtake him.

"I promise," he answered as he lightly kissed my forehead.

We hoisted the bikes over the hood of our car in the trailer and took them with us. Whenever we had a chance, we found trails to explore. We rode through the mountains in Arkansas and east Tennessee.

After a short while, I would tire of the rumbling bike. Brock could ride for hours. He seemed like he had such peace after riding.

We implemented the new stunt we termed "The Blind Ride" into our show. It was a big hit! Word began to spread about this stunt.

****

In the fall of 2002, I contemplated all the places we had been over the last year and a half as I drove our big rig through the streets of Baltimore. We had travelled to Los Angeles, Las Vegas, Portland, Chicago. We had seen the Grand Canyon, Yellowstone National Park, and Niagara Falls. We had driven through the eye of a hurricane in Florida and woken up in the middle of the night to an earthquake in Wyoming.

I was living the adventure I had always wanted, waking up in a new city everyday. So, why did I feel as if something was missing? Sure, it was difficult to find a place to sleep every night. The truck stops were often full and Walmart security guards tended to run us out of the parking lot at 2:00 a.m.

However, this was a minor inconvenience compared to all of the excitement we were experiencing. So, why was I feeling so weary and down lately?

Maybe all of this was too much excitement. How I craved to go to the post office without having to ask for directions. Wouldn't it be amazing to run into someone I knew at the grocery store?

Screeching tires brought me back to my task. Horns began to honk as I saw a van's bumper graze the side of our trailer as we were slowing down for a red light. The roads in the Northeast were much smaller than the rest of the country making it difficult to drive a semi-truck. Somehow, I had crossed over slightly into the van's lane.

I pulled up to the traffic light a few feet away and threw the truck into park. I could not believe that I hit someone. Tears began flooding my eyes as I was overwhelmed with everything.

Brock took my place in the driver's seat and pulled over to the side of the road after the light turned green. He went out to talk with the van owner as I went to the back and laid out on the couch.

Frustration and emotion boiled wildly to the surface. Why was I so distraught over this little fender bender?

After several minutes, Brock entered the back door of the truck and sat beside me.

"It wasn't that big of a deal. The guy didn't have any damage and we only have a small ding on the trailer."

"I don't know what's wrong with me," I said sniffling.

"It's more than a little wreck. You have been more quiet than normal for the last couple of weeks. What's wrong?" he asked as he brushed a tear from my cheek.

"Lately, I feel tired and lonely," I answered between choppy breaths.

"Someone was just telling me the other day that we need to have a house in order to be healthy. We need community and a place to come home to rest. Maybe he is right," he said placing his arm around me.

"Could we afford something like that?" I asked hopefully. "I mean we have to pay monthly for the toterhome."

"I think we could work out something," he said smiling.

A couple of months later, we rented a house in the country outside of Nashville, Tennessee. The location was perfect to travel out of since it was so central to the South and Midwest where the majority of our shows were. Also, many of the Christian bands we shared the stage with lived there, so we already knew some people.

Although we spent more nights in the truck than our house, I still enjoyed having a place to come home to. We attended a church in town and began to meet new people. I quickly learned that hardly anyone was born and raised in Nashville. Everyone was a transplant like us. I felt as if I belonged in this eclectic, artsy community.

When we were in town, we participated in a small group at church. Our group learned about our ministry and began praying for us.

This prayer support would become very valuable to us. We would soon embark upon serious spiritual warfare...

Chapter Six
Calling All Angels

"Your sons and daughters will prophesy, your old men will dream dreams, your young men will see visions." Joel 2:28

I peeked out from behind the curtain as Brock spoke about how Jesus is madly in love with us. I surveyed the crowd in attendance at the small Georgia church. Many senior citizens occupied the first couple of rows. Behind them were several families.

One young man in the back sitting alone caught my attention. He was listening very intently. I noticed a single tear slip down his cheek.

Brock told everyone to close their eyes so they would not be distracted from what God wanted to say. Just then, the man in the back stood up and began walking down the center aisle toward the stage.

What was he doing? Surely he wasn't going to pull out a gun or knife. Curiosity along with a slight nervousness held me frozen in place.

Nobody in the audience did as Brock instructed. They were all watching the man, as intrigued as I was.

Midway down the aisle, he took off his shirt exposing his bare, white chest. One lady with white hair gasped. A boy elbowed his friend pointing to the half naked man.

The guy walked up to the three-foot stage and laid the black t-shirt on it. Then, he fell to his knees on the floor.

Brock picked up the shirt and held it so I could see. The shirt displayed the rapper Eminem holding a bloody chainsaw. I remembered a news report about how controversial this artist was due to his violent lyrics about killing women.

Brock then addressed the rest of the crowd, asking if anyone else would be so bold as the young man. Would they be willing to give up their old lives and old ways to follow Jesus in a new path? Many were moved to action by the physical display of this young man of surrender to God.

Later that night, as we were driving home, I asked Brock, "Who was that guy?" As I was packing up, I noticed Brock giving him one of our t-shirts we had for sale.

He explained that the guy was walking on the sidewalk outside and saw the back doors of the church open. He looked inside shortly after the show began and was interested, so he slipped in the last row.

"So he had never been to that church before?" I asked.

"He has never been to any church before," was his answer.

"Wow! How do we get more people like that at our shows?"

"I've been praying about that very thing, and I think I have the answer. We move our shows from a church building to a neutral location like a civic center or high school auditorium."

"Would the churches still be involved?" I asked with piqued interest.

"Absolutely. Several churches could work together since the venue would not be on anyone's turf. They would be the ones to invite us into their community and pay for it all so that it would be free to the public. We can use our water coffin as a publicity stunt to get people in the door," he said with excitement in his voice.

Hope began to surge as I thought about how the new underwater escape Brock did would make everyone want to come. Being locked and chained in a coffin full of water with windows in it so you could see him at all times was a sight all ages wanted to see. Then, he could deliver the message of how Jesus can take them from spiritual death to life.

****

We immediately implemented the strategy as often as possible with our shows. In addition, Brock began his own tour called the Freedom Experience. This tour consisted of three days of school assemblies promoting the event and then a show each night. We enlisted a BMX freestyle stunt team, freestyle motocross riders, a freestyle skater, and a couple of Christian rock bands to perform with us.

Our attendance went from hundreds to thousands overnight. Also, the demeanor of our audiences changed dramatically. Since the crowd at the neutral venue were usually 80 percent unchurched, they behaved rather wildly.

Over the next year, we had various eye opening displays by audience members. One lady raised her shirt flashing her bare breasts to Brock and the entire crowd. On a different occasion, a girl put both her middle fingers up at Brock as he shared the gospel of Jesus. Once when the emcee was introducing us, a man yelled, "F*** you!" In another instance a fist fight broke out in the third row.

At a show in Wisconsin, Brock was in the middle of his message when a girl in the audience threw her head back and laughed eerily. Immediately, the hairs on the back of my neck stood up. The laugh did not sound human. Brock rebuked her with authority from the stage. Like a light switch turning off, she immediately got quiet and sat up straight.

Every night, Brock had anyone ready to surrender their lives to Jesus to go to a separate room from where the show took place. There, volunteers from the local churches would talk with them about their decision and invite them to come to their church service with them.

On a couple occasions, drug dealers placed the drugs they had on them onto the table in this room renouncing their old lives. Witches gave up the pendant hanging around their neck which was their life line in the Wiccan sect.

A witch came to one of our shows and sat in the back row with voodoo dolls cursing Brock and me as we performed our illusions. When Brock began to passionately share the gospel of Jesus, she passed out in her seat. As soon as his message was over, she woke back up. It was as if she could not bear to hear the words of hope.

In North Carolina the following spring, I overheard some guys talking as I packed up the show we had just completed at a high school. These students had on white t-shirts with the words "Christians not welcome!" written in black marker.

"We are gonna kill some preps tonight!" I heard one of them say.

Quickly I informed Brock and the local church leaders about what was said. They arranged for some police officers to provide security at the event that night.

Minutes before we took the stage, I nervously scanned the audience. It didn't take long to notice the group I had seen earlier. They stood in the center of the high school gym wearing long black trench coats reminiscent of the Columbine school shooters.

"Brock! They could have guns under their coats! I don't think the police officers searched anyone," I exclaimed.

"Well," Brock said peaking from behind the curtain to see the threatening guys, "preaching the gospel of Jesus would not be a bad way to die."

Like most times I felt opposition from the enemy, a righteous anger rose up inside me. This fueled my determination to keep going.

"You're right! Let them kill us! They are not going to stop us from sharing the good news of Jesus," I said passionately.

During the show, the rebellious teenagers stood in a silent protest. They never smiled nor showed any emotion but remained standing for the whole two hours.

Afterwards, I watched as Brock spoke with the guys on the sidewalk outside of the building. They began the conversation by saying they didn't believe God was real. Brock told them he had seen God work in ways that were more than coincidence or luck. He shared our experiences with God providing to the penny what we needed after the trailer was stolen and the truck caught on fire. He told of specific prayer requests answered.

The young men were glued to Brock as he spoke. Their eyes got big after he told of the miraculous events.

"I'd like to pray for you right now," he said.

"Nah, man. I don't want you to," the leader of the group said, his eyes changing from hard cynicism to fear. He motioned to everyone else that they needed to leave.

"For someone who doesn't believe in God, he sure seemed scared to have you pray for him," I said to Brock after they left.

Two weeks later, one of the guys emailed Brock. He couldn't stop thinking about what Brock said to him that night. He eventually went to a church and gave his life to God.

A few months later, we were informed that the leader of the group was arrested. After being tipped off by someone in his group, the police department discovered a list of people he wanted to attack and weapons at his home. He intended to kill people that gathered around the flagpole at school to pray.

****

Weariness settled in as I began to think about the opposition we had faced over the last several months. We had just completed two back-to-back shows and now everything was packed into the trailer this

September night.

I gave a nod to Brock standing in the lobby talking with a few people. "I'll be out there in a minute," he said gently.

A breeze hit me as I opened the door and stepped out into the dark parking lot. I began to hum a song I had heard on the radio as I walked toward our truck.

"I need a sign to let me know You're here," my voice trailed off as I began to think about the words.

"Lord," I prayed stopping to look up at the starry sky. "I feel so worn down. I feel like I do need a sign to help me know You are with us. I need You."

I listened, hoping to get some kind of encouragement from heaven. Looking around the empty lot, all I heard was a bullfrog croaking.

My shoulders slumped as I continued across the pavement. The chorus of the song came to mind and I began to sing, "Calling all angels..."

I slowed my pace and began to think about angels. I wondered about this spiritual realm all around me I couldn't see. What if there were angels right beside me at the moment? What if I wasn't alone on this still night? I sat in the passenger's seat of the truck and continued to ponder spiritual beings.

A few minutes later, Brock opened the door and sat behind the wheel. "Are you ready for this story?"

"Tell me," I said, perking up slightly. I always enjoyed a good story.

He settled back in his seat and told me that a boy about twelve years old came running up to him after the show. The boy was the smart type, dressed nicely, talked intelligently.

He was asking people around him if they had seen them. Then he asked Brock if he felt his hands.

When Brock asked him whose hands he was talking about, he

said, "The angel's!"

Brock encouraged the boy to tell him what he saw. The boy said when Brock was speaking, rows and rows of angels stood behind him. There were too many to count. One big angel towered over Brock's head and had his hands on Brock's shoulders as if guiding his every move. This angel's face was so bright that you could not see it.

"Auny, I am convinced he really saw them. In Joel it talks about our sons having visions," he said shaking his head in amazement.

My heart soared! The Lord had given me my sign through the eyes of a twelve year old boy. He answered my prayer and gave me a glimpse into the supernatural realm.

This had turned my weariness into invigoration! It was good I was rejuvenated. I needed to have energy, because in a few days, we would be on national television.

We were about to discover what live television really meant when we were put on the spot in front of millions of viewers.

CHAPTER SEVEN
Live Television

"For the Holy Spirit will give you the right words at the right time."

Luke 12:12

The following week, I was so excited I could barely contain myself during our show in New Jersey. We were leaving right after the show and driving into New York City.

Earlier that year, we hired a publicist who got us some local news appearances and Christian radio interviews, nothing too major until now. Tomorrow morning, we would be on the *Fox & Friends* morning show which aired nationally on the Fox News Channel.

We had exactly four minutes of air time divided into two segments. We planned to do the blindfolded motorcycle ride through Rockefeller Center and an effect where Brock bent spoons using "the power of his mind." We carefully rehearsed both routines cutting them down to exactly two minutes each.

After we packed up the trailer, we borrowed a local man's pick-up truck figuring it would be easier to drive into the city instead of our toterhome. The large truck was caked with mud. The owner apologized for not having time to clean it up first.

Brock loaded up his bike in the back and we took off. Since it was only our second time to the Big Apple, we entered the wrong end of the island and had to go north several miles before we reached our hotel in Times Square.

Due to the late hour on Saturday night, I figured we would not see much traffic. As I looked around the bustling streets full of cars and pedestrians, I knew my assumption was wrong.

We came to a stop in south Manhattan and I saw four young

women in cocktail dresses sitting in chairs outside of a restaurant. One of the women pointed toward us. The other three looked our way and began laughing.

We began to inch forward in the traffic, and I watched a man in a suit walking along the sidewalk stop and stare at us, a confused expression on his face.

Brock humorously said to him out of his rolled down window, "We took a wrong turn. Where's the dirt bike track?"

The man in the suit smiled and replied, "Not anywhere near here!"

The traffic began to move and we went forward. Brock and I laughed at how ridiculous we looked with a dirty pick-up truck hauling a dirt bike amongst the compact cars driving through the streets of New York City.

When we finally reached the Crowne Plaza three hours later, all of the humor about the situation was gone. We had to be at the Fox News studio in four hours.

Brock pulled into the parking garage. The parking attendant ran out to us shaking his head and yelled in a thick Middle Eastern accent, "You cannot park that thing here!"

"Why not?" Brock asked.

"Because it is too tall and will not fit," the man said annoyed.

I explained that I could ride in the bed of the truck and lay the bike down in order to give enough clearance in the aisle until we got into a spot.

"No, no!" The attendant argued. "I wasn't talking about the bike being too tall. I was talking about the truck. It will not fit under the ceiling of this garage." He wanted us to park the truck with the bike on the street.

Frustration began to build in both Brock and me. Our window for sleep was diminishing.

We had chosen to stay at this particular hotel, despite the high cost, because the producer from *Fox & Friends* suggested it, and we thought it safer to park our dirt bike in a garage rather than on a lot. We certainly did not feel any security about parking it on the street. The bike would probably not be there the next morning.

When I booked the room, the hotel clerk on the phone said it was a good plan. She obviously had not taken into consideration the clearance height of the garage.

"What should we do?" I asked as weariness trumped my irritation.

"You go check us in the hotel and I'll take care of the bike." Brock answered.

I sighed as I walked into the hotel and up the three-story escalator to the lobby.

As I was leaving the desk with our room key in hand, I saw two security guards run by me. I heard a voice sound on one of the men's two-way radios. "There's a bike in the lobby. I repeat! A bike is in the lobby!"

I followed the guards to the escalator. There was Brock holding the handle bars of the bike and propping the frame against his hip, while riding the huge escalator.

At seeing the sight, I began to laugh uncontrollably. The security men were not amused.

Just before Brock reached the top, one of the guards said sternly, "Sir, you cannot bring that up here! What do you think you are doing?"

Brock rolled the bike off the escalator and brought it to a halt. He calmly replied, "The parking attendant told me I couldn't park my bike in the garage, so I guess I'm bringing it to my room."

He explained to the confused security guards that he needed his bike for a television show in the morning. After going back and forth a few times, they came up with a solution. They would store the motorcycle in a broom closet on the first floor.

Since security would not allow Brock to go back down the escalator, he had to put his dirt bike in the elevator. I held the elevator door open as Brock positioned the bike. Giggles began to surface as I saw the bike in the fancy elevator lined with mirrors with classical music playing in the background.

Brock looked at me and said, "It's a crazy life we lead." He grinned as the doors closed.

I took another elevator to the 35th floor to our room. My jaw dropped as I walked in and saw the swanky decor. I looked out the large window overlooking Times Square. It was too bad we only had a few hours to spend in the gorgeous space.

Despite only getting three hours of sleep, I was very enthusiastic as we drove up to the Fox News studio and parked along the curb. We were going to be on national television!

After unloading our gear, we were escorted to a room with a couch and chair facing a television which played the *Fox & Friends* show being taped live in the adjoining room. There was a small table with some breakfast snacks in the corner.

A lady came to take Brock into a dressing room next door to apply television makeup. When Brock hesitated, she explained she would not put lipstick or eyeshadow on him, only powder. The camera tended to make people look pale.

After they exited, I began to munch on a blueberry muffin. "I hate wait," I said to the empty room.

Brock returned after a short while and we waited another 30 minutes. Then, a young woman wearing a headset entered and said she would be taking us out to the street where we would do the first segment.

As we walked outside, I went over the effect we planned to do for the hundredth time. It was almost impossible to make our routines two minutes in length, but we had figured out how to do so and even rehearsed it in our show the previous night.

The hosts, Mike and Juliet, as well as another bystander participated in the first effect. Brock handed each one a spoon on which they wrote their names. Brock placed each spoon in a paper sack.

I got anxious as I realized the one thing we did not take into account in rehearsal. The hosts had microphones and were bantering throughout the routine causing it to take longer.

Brock pulled out a small light bulb and held it with two fingers. Just as he was about to make his next move, I noticed the director standing next to me frantically waving her arms.

Juliet noticed and said, "We have a hard break."

"What's a hard break?" I asked the assistant producer standing near me.

"It means that it will automatically go to commercial," he answered.

"Right now? We cannot hold off for one minute?" I whispered nervously.

"Impossible," he calmly replied.

Juliet explained to the viewers the illusion would continue after a commercial break.

It was a little awkward as we waited for the commercial break to finish. The volunteers still had their paper sacks in hand. However, the hosts of the show laughed and said their audience was used to them doing bizarre things like this.

"And five, four, three..." said the lady to my right.

"And we are back and nothing has happened during the commercial break, I promise," said Mike energetically.

Brock asked everyone to stare at the light bulb. It then exploded into tiny fragments all over the sidewalk.

Gasps rang out from the crowd surrounding us and Juliet jumped.

"We have not looked inside these bags at the spoons yet. Did something happen to them?" Juliet asked.

Brock said, "Take a look and see."

All three people pulled their spoons out of the bags and were so surprised to see that they were now bent and twisted. Brock had not touched their spoons. They had been in the bags the entire time.

Everyone watching began clapping and hollering and I breathed a sigh of relief. We had finished our first segment.

We performed at the end of the show. This part had gone very smoothly. The hosts blindfolded Brock and he jumped on his dirt bike and road through Rockefeller Center dodging big planters and pedestrians.

Then, the hosts began interviewing Brock. He told them he performs at schools, churches, and convention centers all over the country giving them a message of hope and sharing his faith.

I felt a weight lifted off my shoulders. We had completed our two segments.

Then, Juliet said, "Hey, we have time. Why don't you show us one more?"

Panic began to rise in me. We were only supposed to have four minutes total. It had already been ten minutes! I did not plan for any backup because, it seemed impossible. What were we going to do? We were live in front of a million people!

That's when I felt the prayers. A few churches in Texas, Louisiana, and Tennessee were praying for us this Sunday morning. Our small group was at home watching us on the television at that very moment. I knew they were praying.

Our prayers were answered because Brock never looked nervous or at a loss. He simply asked the people who had gathered around out on the sidewalk if any of them had any keys he could use.

One man had a key to spare. Brock took the normal house key and held it in one hand. After concentrating a little while, he opened his hand. The owner of the key gasped. It was now bent.

Everyone else watching began laughing and oohing and awing. It got a better reaction than the planned illusions.

"Whoa!" said Juliet. "And with that we end our show!"

"That's a wrap!" the director said.

We pulled it off! It wasn't easy, but we had made our first national television appearance.

This publicity caused Brock's name to spread. He captured the attention of some prominent people in the Christian entertainment world. It lead to participating in the largest Christian music tour, Winter Jam.

On this tour is where I experienced my most embarrassing moment on a stage.

CHAPTER EIGHT
Two Inches From Death

"Arise, cry out in the night, as the watches of the night begin; pour out your heart like water in the presence of the Lord."
Lamentations 2:19

It was February, 2004. I looked out at the arena seating 8,000 people. Nervousness coursed through my body. After being on the Winter Jam tour for a month, I still had not grown accustomed to the amount of people in the audience each night.

It was exciting sharing the stage with Relient K, Audio Adrenaline, and Todd Agnew. Every night we got in a bunk on a tour bus and were driven to the next city as we slept.

We woke up in a parking garage every morning and followed signs written in marker leading us to our dressing room where we could shower. Catering was usually at the end of the hall down in the bowels of the arena. Everyday of the tour I lived in a concrete city, often times, not seeing the light of day.

On the stage, facing the artist, they had written the city we were in. The venues seemed to look the same and they all ran together. Therefore, we would never know where we were had we not been told.

I tried to make our dressing room, which was a locker room, feel as homey as possible by adding candles and playing music. I carried with me a "happy fun bag." In this bag, I had fiction books to read, the Bible study I was doing at the time, a journal, and a photo album of friends and family.

At first, the tour was exciting, but on this particular night, I was happy we only had a few weeks left. Although it was nice not having to drive ourselves, there was something freeing about the open road ahead of us and being able to stop whenever we pleased. On the bus, we had no control over when and where we stopped.

Brock took the stage, and I watched as he produced card after card from his fingertips. He made 100 cards appear out of thin air.

I was standing behind our next prop getting ready to bring it onstage. It was a big escape that had a 5' X 5' square shaped base with wheels on it and a top with the same diameter. Seven-foot posts stood in the center between the bottom and top. Attached to the posts were stocks that locked in Brock's wrists and legs. Large, leather straps belted him in on each side. A curtain hung from the top and swiveled all the way around the prop.

Each night, I strapped and locked Brock in. Then, I pulled the curtain around him. In less than a second, Brock would emerge from behind the prop completely free of the constraints. When he pulled the curtain back, he revealed me now in Brock's place all buckled and locked in.

Brock would then talk about how we are in bondage to sin. However, just like I took Brock's place in the prop, Jesus took our place on the cross. Anyone could be free if they surrendered to Jesus. The audience seemed to enjoy the speed of the escape and the message that followed.

The crowd applauded as Brock finished his routine. It was time to bring out the monstrous illusion. I looked back and the stagehand that usually got the backside was not in place.

Brock said, "We have a new one for you," as he pointed in my direction.

I smiled as all eyes were on me. I had no choice but to pull the prop out by myself.

I gathered the curtain on the side and placed both hands on the post closest to me. I began to pull scooting backwards. Since people were looking at me, I looked out into the arena and smiled as I attempted to maneuver the awkward contraption around band equipment onto center stage.

I glanced back behind the curtain to see if I had cleared everything. At that moment I saw the back corner of our prop clip the front corner of a keyboard.

Taking my hands off the illusion, I tried to reach for the keyboard, but it was too late. It seemed like slow motion as one keyboard and then another came tumbling to the ground. Pieces of the stand holding the keyboards scattered all over the floor. A few loud clunks sounded as the keyboards hit the ground.

I froze behind the curtain. Panic began to rise inside of me. Did everyone know what just happened? I was behind the curtain on the prop but the keyboards were totally exposed.

"That sounded expensive," I heard Brock say. Everyone began to laugh. Brock continued stalling and cracking jokes for the next few minutes as stage hands ran up collecting the keyboards and pieces.

I stayed behind the curtain. What could I do? We had to do the trick! I couldn't hide behind the curtain all night.

"Okay, Auny! Show them this big thing that's caused so much trouble tonight!" Brock said.

I swallowed my pride and stepped out from behind the curtain. At my appearance, the crowd began to clap. My face was hot, but I forced myself to grin and go on with the show.

After our set, I came out to the table near the entrance of the arena where we sold our t-shirts and DVDs we had of our full-length show. Brock was talking to some teenagers. One of them looked at me and said, "Aren't you the one who knocked down those keyboards?"

"That was me," I said not making eye contact as I slipped behind the table.

The lady who had volunteered to sell our merchandise looked at me and said, "You have sold a lot tonight!"

I quickly added up the money and counted the products. We sold twice as much that night than any other night on the tour!

As I was packing up later, Brock came up to me and said, "I haven't really talked to you after our set."

"That was so embarrassing!" I said letting out a deep sigh.

"It wasn't your fault. I told them before we began that the keyboards were sticking out farther than they usually were."

"Plus, the stage hand didn't help me!" I said exasperated.

Brock grinned and cupped his hand under my chin. "I think you should do that every night. I signed more autographs than I ever have."

"That's only because you had more time onstage and you were cracking jokes up there! It's a good thing you are quick on your feet," I said looking into his eyes.

"I was so proud of you. We are on a different stage each night and have many challenges, worrying about bad angles for certain illusions or large footprints of others. You always do whatever it takes to make the show go on. God made you for this. You are a natural!"

"Even when I crash to the ground expensive instruments?" I asked, feeling comforted by his words.

"Even on your worst night, you are the best," Brock said giving me a quick hug. "Now let's get this packed up and get into our bunks. I'm exhausted."

****

A few months later, during a normal Brock Gill show, silence hung in the air as Brock repeated his demand to the crowd near a teenage boy. "Wake that guy up!"

The fidgeting that had been going on immediately stopped as all 800 students turned around toward the young man in the next to last row. He was slumped in his chair, head hanging to the side, hands crossed in his lap.

A girl sitting next to him gently tapped him on the shoulder. When he did not stir, she placed the palm of her hand on his upper right arm and pushed him firmly, nearly knocking him out of his seat.

He jerked his head up eyes flying open. Looking around, he noticed everyone was looking at him.

"Hey man, I didn't want you to miss what I was going to tell you," Brock said, drawing the attention back to the stage. The teenager nodded and sat up straight in his chair.

I smiled as Brock began to speak. The crowd had been rowdy before he woke the guy up, but now, the only thing you could hear was Brock's voice giving the clear, simple truth about Jesus Christ and His redeeming love.

I remembered the first time I saw Brock display such a bold move. We had only been married a short while and were performing at a show following the high school football game. After Brock had performed his fun, interactive illusions, he got serious and began to speak about Jesus.

A big football player wearing a jersey and jeans entered the back of the room and walked all the way to the front row. He tapped his little brother on the shoulder and motioned to the door.

Brock stopped speaking and pointed straight at the guy. "Hey man," he said gently. "Do you mind taking a seat for a minute?"

I held my breath thinking this large young man might explode with anger. The confrontation made me squirm in my spot backstage. The room was still while everyone waited to see what this tough guy would do.

He shrugged and sat down in an empty chair next to his brother. I let out a sigh of relief.

From behind the curtain, I kept my eyes on the ball player as

Brock continued his message. His eyes softened as he listened closely.

Brock gave an opportunity for anyone who was thinking about giving their lives to Jesus to leave the room in order to talk with someone from the church about it. I watched as the guy quickly wiped away a tear and stood up responding to the invitation. He surrendered his life to Jesus that night.

I learned to never question Brock's authority when he was sharing the gospel of Jesus. He often broke the rules. Whenever the audience wasn't listening, he would speak quieter. Often times, he would pause, silence hanging in the air for an uncomfortable amount of time. However, it worked. With the amount of unchurched people in our audience, it was fortunate that Brock knew how to handle a disorderly crowd. He seemed to win them over every time.

I peaked out at the still assembly. This night was no exception. Chills formed on my arms as I watched many respond to the invitation to follow Christ.

After we packed up and said our goodbyes, we sat down in the cab of the truck. "I'm not sure how far I can get tonight. That show wore me out," Brock said wearily.

We were in Houston, Texas and were planning to drive as far as we could that night and stay at a truck stop. Then, the drive home the next day would not be so long.

"Let me drive," I offered, still having leftover adrenaline from doing a show.

After driving for half an hour, I turned onto a two lane dark highway on the north side of Houston. I glanced over at Brock who was staring out the window.

The high from the show began to wear off, and I started crashing down. I yawned as I looked out at the desolate stretch of road.

I turned to Brock to try and enlist his help in staying awake. He was peering intensely out in front of us. His face was colored with concern.

Jerking my eyes to where Brock was looking, I saw a flash of headlights. In an instant, a shotgun blast pierced the night! The windshield splattered and glass fragments flew through the air!

I eased up, taking my foot off the accelerator and gripping the steering wheel. The truck began to gradually slow down.

Quickly, I assessed my body. I didn't feel any pain. Was I shot? Maybe I was in shock and that's why I couldn't feel anything hurting. Was I dead?

"Put your foot on the brake and pull over," Brock instructed, snapping me out of my frozen state. I eased the big rig off onto the shoulder and turned off the engine.

Brock jumped out of the truck and I picked up our cell phone from the dash and called 9-1-1.

"What's your emergency?" a young girl with a southern accent answered.

I briefly contemplated what to say. I didn't know what happened. A few minutes ago, I was driving peacefully down the road.

"I think we've been shot!" I blurted out my voice high pitched and strained.

She took down my location. "We don't have anyone available at this time," she said calmly.

"What do you mean?" I asked frantically.

"All of our officers are out on a call right now. I'll send them as soon as I can."

After getting off the line, I joined Brock outside. I observed the windshield. A football sized hole was above the driver's seat along the top of the window. The glass was spider webbed from that hole extending the length and width of the pane.

I informed Brock that a police officer would come whenever one was free from their current duty.

"I saw three pick-up trucks in the oncoming lane when this happened," Brock said pointing up to the fragmented windshield. "I think there were guys standing up in the back of them."

At that moment, I heard diesel engines approaching. I leaned out to the side of our totorhome to see a few trucks barreling toward us in our lane. "Those are the trucks I saw!" Brock yelled.

I ran back into the truck and watched as one by one, they pulled to the side of the road a few feet in front of us. "Get in the truck!" I screamed to Brock, but he could not hear me due to the screeching tires of the vehicles.

He stood with his fists clenched, looking like he was ready to fight. I silently prayed for the Lord to intervene.

I could not make out faces, but I counted five heads in the third truck alone. We were totally outnumbered and there was nobody else in sight. There were not any houses or buildings to take cover, only woods on both sides.

If Brock would get in the truck, maybe we could just drive. However, these trucks could outrun our sixteen ton Freightliner and trailer. Maybe we should hide out in the woods. Then the culprits might vandalize or steal our truck, but we might be safe. Were these guys going to kill us?

Just when I was about to make a move, headlights from the oncoming lane approached. As the car passed, the lead truck took off back onto the road. The other two followed. I breathed a sigh of relief when they were out of sight.

Picking up the phone, I nervously called 911 again. The same operator answered.

I desperately explained that the guys who had shot at us came back by. "Ma'am, I will send somebody to you as soon as possible," she answered curtly.

"Okay," I said and then ended the call.

My fear began to change to anger. I was angry that the 9-11 operator was rude instead of helpful. I was angry that no police officers were available when we needed them, and I was angry that this random act of violence happened to us in the first place!

"Lord, how can you let stuff like this happen to us? Theft, fire, and now this?" I yelled in the empty truck. The theft and fire were devastating, but this was different. We could have been killed!

The words of a scripture from John floated across my heart, "In this world, you will have trouble. But take heart! I have overcome the world."

I took several short breaths trying to calm down. Tears began to surface as the realization of what happened set in.

The back door opened and Brock said, "There is glass all the way back here!"

I stepped into the living quarters and heard a crunch under my shoes. I noticed glass particles down the aisle between the couch and table all the way to the back wall.

"Judging by the hole in the windshield and the two dents in the trailer, it looks as if they threw something at us," he said shaking his head.

"It sounded like gunfire," I commented.

"A brick flying at 70 miles per hour could have that kind of impact."

"Is that what you think it was?" I asked weary from the roller coaster of emotions I had experienced over the last several minutes.

"That would be my guess," he answered.

"Is the trailer bad?"

"Nah, the windshield is definitely worse."

We both sat down on the couch. Brock called 9-11 and spoke with the girl. "She's not in a hurry," he said after he hung up.

"Not at all," I said feeling defeated.

"Right before those trucks approached, I felt like I needed to pray for our protection," he said putting his arm around me. "It looks like whatever it was, it hit more of the frame of the truck than the window. If it had been a couple of inches lower, it would have come through the window and right into your face."

I leaned into his shoulder and closed my eyes. I wondered if Brock's prayer saved my life. I escaped death by only two inches.

After waiting for another hour and calling the police a few more times, we left. Due to the dramatic turn of events, we decided to stay with my parents who lived an hour away instead of driving to a truck stop. I really needed a hug from my mom.

Brock sat at an angle where he could see through the cracks, and began to drive. A few miles down the road, we saw a police car sitting in a driveway of a large house.

We pulled over to the side of the road and jumped out. A police officer in uniform got out of the car and walked to meet us.

We explained what had happened and that we were waiting for the police to come for over an hour and nobody came.

"I am so sorry about that. It's not usually like this. I am off duty working a private event, but I'll take a report since you have not been helped tonight," the man said gently.

He went to his car and retrieved a clipboard with paper and pen. He began to write as we gave him a detailed description of what happened. Then, he walked to the front of our truck and began writing his observations concerning the windshield.

"You were driving?" he asked me.

After I nodded, he patted me on the shoulder and said, "Someone up above was looking out for you. That was a close one!"

He told us that this same type of violence had occurred the previous weekend. Three trucks came by a man driving a pick-up truck. They had a guy in the back of each truck who threw a cinder block at him as they drove by. It ran him off the road. The boys in the trucks came back by and stopped on the shoulder near the crashed truck. They beat the victim with baseball bats and left him for dead. He barely survived.

"Why do you think they didn't beat us?" Brock asked.

"It sounds like the oncoming car scared them off. I'm telling you! You two were lucky! Do you want to drive to the police station and talk with someone there?" the officer said.

"I'm ready to go to my parents house and go to bed. It's been a long night," I answered, looking at Brock.

The officer promised us that he would file the report first thing in the morning. We thanked him and left. I was in bed asleep an hour later.

A few days after the incident, as I was cleaning my house in Tennessee, my thoughts kept drifting back to driving on that dark road that night. I replayed the sound and glass spraying everywhere over and over.

As I vigorously dusted the end table in the living room, my mind flashed back to college. Gin always cleaned when she was stressed. Our apartment style dorm was spotless during finals week.

I put down the cloth in my hand and picked up my cell phone and dialed Gin. I realized it had been months since we had talked.

She answered on the third ring. We caught up on the last few months. Then, I told her about my near death experience.

"Wait a second," Gin interrupted. "Did this happen Friday night?"

"Yes. How did you know?" I asked.

"I was asleep Friday night...like long gone asleep. The Lord woke me up and told me to pray for you."

"What?" I could not believe it.

"Yeah," Gin continued. "Honestly, I have not prayed for you in a while, so I thought it was interesting that the Lord brought you to mind. I wasn't having a dream about you or anything. It was like out of the blue! It felt like the Lord shook me awake to get me to pray for you. I prayed for an hour or so and went back to sleep. I kept meaning to call you and ask about it, but I would forget. I figured if something big happened, I'd hear about it."

"Well, something big happened!" I was so grateful to Gin to heed that calling to pray. So many people would have just gone back to sleep.

We talked a little longer, both amazed at how the Lord worked in this situation.

After hanging up the phone, I sat on the sofa and looked up to the ceiling toward heaven. A warm sensation worked its way through my body and up to my face. I smiled and said, "Lord, you woke someone from the dead of sleep to pray for me."

A feeling of safety that had been missing since the drama returned. God was looking out for me.

Gin was a prayer warrior. Everyone close to her knew it. Sometimes when I came home from work or school, Gin would say, "I felt led to pray for you about ____ today." It would be just what I had needed or was thinking that day. It was incredible the way she interceded in prayer.

I had interceded for people in the past. Whenever someone asked me to pray for them, I faithfully did so. However, I never prayed as fervently as Gin.

After the phone call, I was inspired to pray the Lord would choose me to intercede on behalf of others in the future. I wanted to be the one who the Lord woke up in the middle of the night to battle in prayer on someone's behalf. A few months later, my prayer was answered.

The Lord called on me to intercede for two ladies.

CHAPTER NINE
Ministry at Home

"I looked for a man among them who would build up the wall and stand before me in the gap." Ezekiel 22:30

In the fall of 2004, we purchased a little wooden house out in the country south of Nashville. It was eighteen hundred square feet and sat on four acres of hilly, rocky ground with several mature trees.

Gratitude filled my heart when I stepped into our new house for the first time. Growing up, we lived in houses designated for the pastor. We never owned a house. It was a dream of mine to buy a house, but I never expected to actually get it.

I walked around each room and prayed over them. When I went into the guest bedroom, I paused.

"Lord, you are allowing us to manage this house, but it is Yours. I want to open it up to whomever you wish to stay here or live here. I pray that when people enter this home, they will experience You...that Your light will fill it! I want people to feel loved and accepted when they come in here."

I walked into the kitchen, through the dining room, and over to the master bedroom. It was on the other end of the house connected by a narrow room we were using as a dining room. I noted the house was set up well to have guests since our bedroom was separate from the rest of the house and completely private.

We could have people who travel stay with us! Maybe someone could even live with us. This could be a new ministry opportunity. Excitement about all the possibilities sprang up inside of me.

I searched for Brock to tell him my idea concerning opening up our house. He was standing on the back porch looking out to our grassy hill leading up to woods. When I opened the back door, I realized he was talking on the phone.

Listening, I tried to guess who he was talking with. It was a game I liked to play. About sixty percent of the time, I was able to correctly name the person on the other end of the phone simply by analyzing Brock's choice of words plus the tone as he spoke.

I could hear a man's voice on the other line. He sounded extremely energetic.

Brock said goodbye and ended the call. Turning to me he said, "You are never going to believe who that was!"

"I tried to figure it out but couldn't. He sounded very spirited. Who was it?"

He put his hands on my shoulders and squeezed. "That was Stephen Baldwin!"

"The actor?" I asked.

"Yes! He came to know the Lord after 9/11."

"Why did he call you?" I asked curiously.

Brock explained that Stephen had teamed up with the Luis Palau association and was doing a tour all over the country called "Livin It." They were using action sports teams and Steven would speak. They wanted Brock to speak as well.

"That's great! When do we start?" I asked eagerly.

"Well, that's the only issue. They only want me to do one effect and then get right into the gospel. Also, they will fly me to every city."

"So, I am not invited," I said disappointed.

"It's going to be a bunch of guys. You wouldn't enjoy it anyway," he said placing his hand on my back and rubbing it gently.

"Is it a lot of dates?" I asked, trying pretty hard to regain the enthusiasm I possessed a few minutes prior.

"It's only twelve dates beginning in a few weeks. The other hundred or so shows we do in the next year, you will be apart of. I promise."

Brock's phone began to ring. He held up a finger indicating that we needed to put our conversation on hold and answered it.

I looked out into our backyard and thought about spending twelve nights alone here while Brock was off having adventures and seeing great ministry.

I had purpose when we did shows and shared the gospel. I lived for those moments when I saw God work in people's lives. He used us to accomplish it.

My prayer from earlier came back to me. I had asked God to bring ministry to our house. Maybe God could use me at home, too.

"Lord, please, use me here. I'm willing to do anything You want. Please, help me to cultivate friendships. Use this time at home to grow me and help others."

****

It was the third night of the "Livin It" tour and I was eating dinner with some friends at a restaurant in our hometown. One of the girls eating with me asked, "What do you do when Brock's out of town?"

All of a sudden, I felt anger begin to burn inside of me. Something about the question set me on edge. Why was I feeling so defensive? It was a simple question.

Heat began to rise to my face. I made myself calmly reply, "Usually I go with him everywhere. This tour is a one time thing. I'll be right back," I said excusing myself.

In the hallway, outside of the bathroom, I called Brock. Quickly into the conversation he asked, "What's wrong?"

I told him the question I was just asked and the anger it ensued. "What do you think made you feel that way? Was it that she didn't understand you and your lifestyle?"

I thought about what Brock said. This was a common problem. It was easier to find people in Nashville who understood what we did better than other parts of the country simply because many of them were somehow involved with Christian bands. However, we were very different from bands. Most of them consisted of men. Their wives usually stayed home. We were not like this. I went on the road just as much as Brock...until now.

"I think I got defensive because it made me feel lazy," I said digging down to the depths of what I felt when the question was presented. "You are out working and doing ministry, and I am not."

"Auny," Brock said his voice softening to almost a whisper. "You are the hardest worker in show business. Everyone on the road knows that. I only have a short set on this tour, but it still takes three people to do what you do by yourself every show. If anyone deserves a break, it's you." His voice rose and filled with passion as he said, "That's a lie from Satan to think you are not doing anything for the Kingdom if you are not with me on the road. Did you pray for me earlier today when I spoke?"

"Of course!" I answered, my spirit beginning to lift.

"Okay, then. The people at home may never know how hard you work, but I do. God does, and you are being obedient by going with me and by staying home this time. He has a reason for you to be at home right now, I'm sure of it!"

I felt encouraged as I hung up the phone and joined my friends back at the table. After dinner, I headed toward my car. The sun was just beginning to set causing the clouds to take on a brilliant orange. I looked across the large parking lot to the bookstore 50 yards away. I needed a new book, so I decided to walk over there on this nice evening.

I passed my truck and made my way to the Borders bookstore. My phone began to ring, so I stopped and retrieved it from my pocket.

Brock's voice held much concern when he spoke on the other end. "I just talked to Ben. He's playing guitar with Joy Williams in New York tonight. Kara is at home. She just found out she lost the baby."

My heart sank. Ben and Kara were friends we had met in our small group at church. They moved to the area at the same time we did. Since their family was in Colorado and our family was in Texas, we had Thanksgiving together the previous year. We tried to spend time with them as much as possible when we were home and Ben was not traveling. The four of us celebrated when we found out Kara was pregnant with their first child.

"She must be devastated! And she's all alone," I said. I quickly ended the call with Brock and dialed Kara's number. As I dialed, I continued to walk toward the bookstore.

It was ringing, "Come on, Kara, pick up," I said, aching to put my arms around her and comfort her right now.

"Hello?" Kara said tentatively.

"Hey, this is Auny," I began.

"I know where you are," she said.

"What?" I stopped walking and looked around confused.

"You're in the parking lot of Borders bookstore. I know because I'm sitting in the same parking lot," said Kara.

I searched around for her car and there she was just a few feet away. She was standing by the driver's seat with the door open.

Even from where I stood, I could see the sadness in her eyes and the way her shoulders were slumped.

I hung up the phone and ran to her.

"I'm glad you're here because," she began saying.

"I know," was my answer as I pulled her into an embrace.

She began sobbing, her delicate shoulders shaking with grief and pain. I was crying too as I imagined how devastated she must have felt.

After staying there for some time weeping, I said, "Come on. I'll buy you coffee."

We went to the bookstore café, got some coffee, and found a table back in the corner providing some privacy.

Kara explained, "The Lord sent you at the right time and put you in the right place."

I waited as she sipped her coffee and brushed away a couple of tears.

"I was driving around aimlessly. I cried out to the Lord telling Him I did not want to go home and I did not want to be alone...not tonight. I drove into this parking lot and parked not really knowing what to do. Next thing I know, I see you walking by at the same time my phone rings and your name is on my caller ID."

I let that settle on my heart. The Lord certainly wanted me to be right where I was at this moment. Brock was right. The Lord did have a reason for keeping me home at this time.

We talked in the coffee shop for a long time. Healing would take some time, but at least Kara did not have to be alone on day one. Her husband would be home the next day, so they could grieve together.

Now that the Lord had called on me to comfort one of his children, I was addicted. I wanted to be there for more people in their time of need.

I had no idea that the next opportunity would come a few weeks later.

****

I smiled as I stepped over the mattress on the floor in the dining room. The BMX stunt team from Wisconsin who had participated in the event we put together called the Freedom Experience were staying at our house for a couple of weeks between shows. The leader traveled with his wife and two young boys. Plus there were three additional riders.

"Hey Jen! Where are the guys?" I asked the leader's wife who was pouring some milk for her son in the kitchen.

"They are at the skatepark riding," she answered as she handed her one-year old a sippy cup.

"Well, I am going into town to have lunch with a couple of girls from church. Do you want to go? You can bring the boys," I said kneeling down to the boy and kissing his chubby cheek.

"Nah. I've already begun making lunch and I'm excited about having some alone time when I put them down for their nap."

"Alone time is such a rare thing for people living on the road like us. Enjoy it!" I told her as I walked out the door.

A few minutes later, I was sitting at a table at a restaurant with Heather and Susan. When the waitress set down our sandwiches, Susan looked at me and asked if I would say the blessing.

"Sure!" I said as they bowed their heads. "Lord, let the three of us have a great talk here today. Help us to grow closer to You and each other. And thanks for the food. See ya!" I froze, embarrassed as I realized that I didn't say the typical "amen."

Susan smiled and said, "Peace out, God!"

The three of us laughed.

Susan said, "That's why I asked you to pray. You always seem so genuine when you pray like you're just talking with your best friend."

"I'm glad you said that. I always feel a little funny praying out loud just because I think of it as such an intimate thing," I commented.

"I need prayer right now," Heather interjected. "My doctor just told me something's wrong with the baby. I think I might have to spend the last five months of my pregnancy in bed."

"What's wrong?" Susan asked with concern.

"He might not make it," Heather said tears surfacing.

At that moment, I heard the Holy Spirit whisper to me, "Heather's baby is fine, but Susan is not." I looked down at my plate. "Lord, did I hear you correctly? What's wrong with Susan?"

"Auny?" Susan asked snapping me back into the conversation. "Don't you think we need to pray for Heather's baby?"

"Of course," I answered pushing my strange thoughts to the side and focusing on the company at hand. We continued our meal and learned more about Heather and her baby's health.

I did not think about this comment I heard from the Lord until a couple of weeks later when I saw Heather. She and her husband were worship leaders and happened to be at the same event we were performing and speaking at in North Carolina.

Heather ran up to me smiling and threw her arms around me. "The doctor made a mistake. My baby's fine!" She said after her embrace.

She explained that she had seen another doctor and after two more sonograms, they believed the baby was normal and healthy.

I rejoiced with her, but in the back of my mind I remembered the exact words I heard that day at lunch. If Heather's baby was indeed "fine," then where did that leave Susan?

After we were done with our show that evening, I slipped out of the conference center a little early and went back to our hotel room. Brock was still hanging out with our friends and some students. This was fine with me because I needed to process what I had learned.

Did this mean Susan was in trouble? Susan was not pregnant, so maybe it meant she had some physical problems. I was so confused on what to pray, but I knew the Lord was calling me to pray for Susan.

I began praying harder than I ever had before. This was a life I was praying for! This was a sweet, Godly woman. I did not want anything bad to happen to her. I literally got on my knees and then all the way down on the floor in my hotel room battling in prayer like never before.

A couple of weeks later, we were eating dinner with Susan and her husband, Rod. They were extra bubbly that night and we soon found out why. Susan was pregnant.

Alarm bells went off in my head. Maybe the message was about Susan's baby. Maybe it was referring to Susan, maybe both!

When I got home that night, I took a shower. I usually take a shower in the mornings, but I just needed to think. I was so distraught about this message I heard from the Lord that I felt physically ill.

As the steam filled my senses, a thought came to me. In Genesis, after Abraham pleaded with God concerning Lot, God changed His mind. Maybe He could do that in this situation. He could change His mind, because at this point, I was convinced something bad was going to happen to Susan and the baby.

I prayed for Susan everyday. It was so intense when I prayed for her that often times I cried out in desperation or sobbed uncontrollably.

One day, Brock walked in on me crying. He came running to my side holding me and asking me what was wrong. Brock wanted to know the problem so that he could solve it.

"You cannot fix this one. I don't even know what the problem is exactly." I then told him what I heard and what I felt. Brock began praying with me for Susan. It helped to share this heavy burden with someone.

We couldn't tell anyone else. People would think we were crazy!

I could not explain it, but I knew I had heard from God. There was a fervency to my prayers when it came to Susan that could only come from Him.

About four months into Susan's pregnancy, we went on vacation with her and Rod. On the day we left for the trip, she was going to have a sonogram which would tell her if she was having a girl or a boy. It would also indicate if the baby had any problems.

We took separate flights to get there, so I did not know the results of Susan's sonogram yet. I was so anxious. What if the sonogram showed something was terribly wrong with the baby and the Lord knew we would be on a trip together when they found out? Maybe He wanted to give me a heads up, so I could comfort them better.

When I saw Susan that day, I was about to burst. "How was your doctor visit?" I couldn't wait another minute to ask.

"Well..." Susan drew out the news. Then, she smiled and said, "It's a girl!"

I sighed in relief and then hugged her. Her name was going to be "Anna."

My prayers for Susan did not decrease after hearing everything was good at her checkup. They just changed a little. Now, I was praying for Susan and Anna.

Several months later, around the time Susan was due, I had an urgent feeling to pray for her at that moment. I called her and she did not answer her phone. I tried again, and she still didn't answer.

"Okay, breathe," I told myself. She was probably in labor and couldn't answer the phone, but that did not mean anything was going wrong with the labor. However, I could not shake the foreboding, bad feeling.

Since we were on the road, I could not drive to her house or the hospital. I was so frustrated. I tried calling probably a half dozen more times. Brock tried calling Rod but could not get hold of him. I kept telling myself something my mother always said, "No news is good news."

That night during our show, I was distracted. I could only think of Susan and Anna. I also began praying for Rod, Susan's parents, the doctors...everyone who I thought was involved.

I did not sleep very well that night. When I woke up several times, my thoughts were always on Susan.

The next day, as we were driving to our next show, I told Brock to try calling Rod again. Rod answered! I could see Brock smiling and nodding. This was a good sign. Brock offered a quick congratulations and got off the phone.

Brock said, "She had the baby and she and Anna are doing fine."

Wow! Maybe I was wrong about what I had heard, or maybe the Lord did change His mind. I was so relieved after praying so diligently for months.

It was not until a week later that I found out what really happened. Susan had gone to the doctor for a check-up. They told her that her blood pressure was too high and they needed to deliver the baby right then. They rushed her to the hospital to do a c-section. None of the anesthesia took for her. Other complications arose. Doctors were doing everything they could.

When they delivered Anna, she did not even cry because she was so lethargic due to the drugs they had to give Susan. They rushed Anna to ICU and continued working on Susan.

After a little attention, they were able to save Anna. However, they were losing Susan.

At some point during this, Susan's dad told Rod he and the baby could live with him. The truth was Susan was dying.

Then, by some strange turn of events, Susan's body began to fight for life. The doctors were working hard to save her and a miracle happened. Susan lived. After it seemed like it was done, her life on this earth was over, the Lord stepped in and saved her.

When I learned the reality of what happened and almost happened on the day Anna was born, I wept knowing the Lord entrusted me with two of his treasures, Susan and Anna. He called on me to battle in prayer for them. It was a battle. I had never prayed that hard in my life! For ten months, I was consumed with Susan and her baby.

A few weeks after Anna was born, I was able to sit down with Rod and Susan and tell them all that had happened in my prayer life. Susan cried and I cried. The battle was over!

It felt so gratifying to hold baby Anna in my arms. She was alive and so was Susan!

Our friendship with them deepened after this connection through prayer the Lord had orchestrated.

Rod was the Vice President and Susan worked in Artist Development at Word Entertainment, one of the leading Christian music labels in the country. They supplied us with artists for the Freedom Experience. Rod enlisted Brock to perform at some of the Word artist showcases.

Rod and Susan quickly became some of the biggest encouragers of our ministry. We would need all the support we could get in the coming months.

Our ministry was about to spread to millions around the world by way of television.

CHAPTER TEN
As Seen on TV

"And pray in the Spirit on all occasions with all kinds of requests." Ephesians 6:18

I jolted awake from my bed above the cab as our truck came to a stop. Rubbing my eyes, I wondered how long I had been napping. I peeked out the tiny window above my bed to see we were at a truck stop. This particular one in Birmingham, Alabama was very familiar since we came through there often.

Brock was talking to Duane, the guy we had hired to help us out with our heavy tour schedule during the spring of 2005. The truck dipped to the right and to the left after Brock and Duane got out of the vehicle.

I stretched my arms above my head. I needed to go to the restroom. Instead of using the bathroom in our totorhome, I decided to take a walk and use the one in the store.

I glanced out at Brock who had just begun to pump the fuel in one of our 100 gallon tanks. This would take several minutes, so I slipped out of the back door and made my way into the truck stop.

Halfway there, I realized I had left my cell phone in the truck. I shrugged thinking I would not be long and continued on to the entrance.

It was a nice, sunny day. I had a little spring in my step as I walked inside. The nap had rejuvenated me. After doing back to back Freedom Experiences, I needed to sleep for a week to catch up.

Our days during this event looked like this: leave for a school assembly at 7:00 a.m., set up sound system and illusions to perform, and then tear down three times during the day, grabbing lunch somewhere in between. After our last school assembly, we began our four-hour setup for the night show.

Then, we performed the show which lasted two hours. I directed the entire event which meant I made sure everything went smoothly for the bands and action sports guys. By the time it was our turn to be onstage, I was exhausted. After the show, we tore down our equipment. We repeated this the next day for three days.

As I headed back toward our big rig, I thought about all the people in attendance and how many responded to the gospel of Jesus, over 2,500 showed up on the last night alone and hundreds came to Christ.

All of the hard work and lack of sleep was worth it. I sighed with satisfaction.

Our truck began to pull forward. I assumed Brock would stop just beyond the pump and park as he normally did.

I frowned as I noticed it was going rather quickly. Instead of stopping, it picked up speed.

Brock was not aware I had stepped out of the vehicle. I began to run toward the 16 ton beast which was moving very fast. I could hear the powerful engine being put in high gear. If I didn't catch up, I'd be left here with no cell phone. How long would it take for Brock or Duane to discover I was not sleeping in the back?

Sprinting faster, I finally reached the passenger side of the living quarters and banged on the wall with the palm of my hand. The truck began to slow and I saw Duane noticed me in the side mirror.

I slowed my pace to a brisk walk trying to catch my breath. The passenger door flew open and Duane motioned for me to come.

As the truck was still moving, I ran toward the open door. Duane lifted me by my arms into the cab.

I watched as Brock put his hands on the wheel and pushed down the accelerator. His jaw was tense in determination.

"What's going on?" I asked, throwing myself on the floor between

Brock and Duane.

"There were some guys up to no good there. I think they were trying to steal our truck!" Brock answered.

After he drove out of the parking lot and back onto the interstate, he breathed a sigh of relief. Then, he looked at me and asked, "What were you doing? I thought you were still in the back!"

"I went to the bathroom in the truck stop. I know I should have told you, but I had just woken up and wasn't thinking clearly. I thought I'd be back before you left. I promise, I won't do that again."

I looked over at Duane and then Brock. "Now will someone tell me why you turned this Freightliner into a race car?"

They both excitedly plunged into the story. A man approached Brock while he was pumping fuel. He asked him about our truck. It was common for people to ask about it since toterhomes were rare.

Then, the stranger told Brock to drive back to an area behind some parked trucks. A truck driver had won the big lottery and the local news station was present capturing the man's story.

Brock, who had a knack for reading people, sensed the man was lying. He fueled up as quickly as possible and tried to get the guy to back off. Instead, the man became more persistent. When Brock got back into the truck the guy aggressively hung on his side mirror standing on the step as Brock began to move the truck forward.

He drove faster forcing the man to release his grip and jump back to the ground. At that moment, he heard knocking on the other side of the truck. He feared it was another guy in on the attempted theft until Duane spotted me in the mirror.

Brock's phone rang and he answered, adrenaline still sounding in his voice. It was a friend who lived in Birmingham. Brock told him the story of what just happened at the truck stop near where his friend lived.

"You are not going to believe this!" Brock said after ending the call. "He just told me there is no lottery in this state!"

"What do you think that man was trying to pull?" Duane asked.

"I saw some men standing in the direction the guy was pointing. I think he wanted to get us in the very back of the parking lot so they could carjack us," he answered.

We talked about it for awhile going over all the scenarios that could have taken place that day.

After several minutes, Duane went to the back to rest and I took his seat in the passenger's chair.

When we were alone, Brock said, "I wanted to talk to you about something."

I listened carefully as he continued, "I've been praying about doing a television special."

"You mean like we did on *Fox & Friends*?" I asked.

"No something bigger like what David Copperfield and David Blaine have done."

"Wow! That would be huge, but they have big networks and sponsors backing them. We don't have connections like that," I pointed out.

"That's true, but I really have a desire to do it."

"Let's pray about it. God has more connections than anyone in the world," I said looking out the window and up at the blue sky.

"So, you want to pray that an opportunity comes to us? You don't think we should make something happen?"

"The only way to 'make something happen' would be to go to Los Angeles and knock on people's doors. I wouldn't know where to start. Plus, we are so busy on the road. We don't have time to make it happen." I looked at Brock's disappointed face and said, "If God wants you to do a TV special, He will orchestrate it."

"You are right," he said sounding hopeful. "And it will be the right TV show."

I looked back up at the sky and began to fervently pray this would happen.

****

Two days later, Brock received a phone call. I looked over at him from the hotel bed where I was sitting reading a book.

His face became animated as he talked. He looked at me and mouthed, "You are never going to guess who this is," as he pointed to the cell phone.

After the call ended. He looked at me and said, "That was the British Broadcasting Company. They want me to be in a documentary about the miracles of Jesus!"

I jumped off the bed! "So it will air in British Columbia?"

"Better! It's going to be aired on the Discovery Channel all over the world!"

I ran to Brock sitting in a chair and put my hands on his cheeks. "You got your TV special!"

"I know! God didn't waste any time answering that prayer request!"

"How did they find you?" I asked, sitting on the edge of the bed.

"I'm not sure. They told me they wanted a Christian magician because they are exploring the idea of Jesus being a magician. Apparently a lot of people think that Jesus was using magic and disguising it as miracles. I'm going to help prove He did real miracles."

"That's perfect!" I said clapping my hands.

"Will you get paid?" I asked him.

"A little, but not much. I would do it for free if I had to. Can you imagine how many people across the world it will touch?"

****

A week later, Brock was on a plane going to a water studio in Malta, an island in the Mediterranean. On this stage, they filmed Titanic and many other movies with ocean scenes.

For a week, the BBC filmed Brock calming the sea by using modern day technology. The storm was created with large wind machines. When Brock yelled, "Stop!" They simply turned off the machines.

A month after that, Brock flew to Israel and filmed most of the other scenes. The film crew came to the United States and filmed us during a few shows to finish off the program. The documentary cost ten million dollars to film which was the most expensive Christian documentary made to date.

We gathered at some friends house from church on Christmas, 2005 to view the airing of *The Miracles of Jesus*. Half of our small group watched the three-hour special with us. We received phone calls from all over the country of others who were doing the same.

Brock was in almost every scene, interviewing people and performing illusions. He convincingly showed the only explanation for the miraculous stunts Jesus displayed was He was the Son of God.

After *Miracles of Jesus* aired, our popularity increased. Our schedule doubled and the distance we traveled expanded.

****

As we boarded a plane to go home in the spring of the following year, I thought about all the exciting places we had been over the last few months... Washington DC, Rhode Island, Massachusetts, Maine,

Vermont, Miami and Florida.

Our publicist knew someone who got us into Disney World for free while we were there. We flew straight from Florida to Alaska.

There, we performed nine shows in three days. The four-hour time change was brutal.

I put my hand over my mouth as I yawned. It was good we had a smaller show when we flew. I could not have handled nine big shows with a four-hour set up for each. There were not enough hours in the day.

When we flew to shows, we used practical items such as spoons, light bulbs, and playing cards which could be purchased at any store across the country. Brock also used items people in the audience had with them. For example, he linked together three wedding bands taken from audience members' hands. He would bend a few keys he had collected from people's pockets like he did on *Fox & Friends*. With the aid of a video camera, large crowds could clearly see what was happening onstage.

"You tired?" Brock asked as we inched our way down the jet bridge.

"I am," I answered with a sigh. "After three weeks being gone, I'm so ready to be home. I actually was homesick yesterday."

"You? Homesick?" Brock said surprised. "Even though you are checking off your list of all the states and going on so many adventures?"

"I know it's not like me."

"Well, you have a whole week before we have to leave again," Brock said putting his hand on my back.

"I will probably say I'm going to go home and sleep all week. Then, I will do what I always do. Come two o'clock tomorrow, I'll be ready to get out of the house."

The line began to move and we sat down in our seats. I was

grateful there were only two seats on the right side of the plane. This allowed Brock to sit on the aisle and me by the window.

I got settled and looked out of the window on my right. "Now, you can relax," I told myself.

At that point, I felt something inside my body release. Pain shot up through my stomach and into my chest. It was as if hot lava had been dumped into my bloodstream and was coming up into my throat.

My face got hot and the walls of the small plane began to close in on me. As the plane began to jolt into action, I laid both arms across my stomach and buckled over.

"Auny, what's wrong?" Brock asked concerned.

I glanced his direction and tried to speak, but nothing would come out.

"You have gone extremely pale."

"I don't know what's wrong," I groaned. "I feel like I'm going to pass out and throw up all at the same time."

The plane lifted off the ground and my stomach began to churn. Brock put his hand on my back and began gently stroking me.

After thirty minutes, Brock whispered, "Lay your head against the wall and rest. You are probably extremely tired."

I nodded and did as he suggested. For the next four hours, I closed my eyes and tried to go to sleep.

However, my body was in such turmoil that I could not relax. I was very tense thinking at any moment, the reindeer sausage I had for breakfast would come up.

When we landed in Minneapolis, Brock suggested eating something might help settle my stomach. I felt a little better after walking around a bit, so I decided to try some Asian food.

As soon as we sat at a table with our rice dish in hand, the walls began closing in on me. My face grew hot again. I could feel my eyes closing and my body slipping down in the chair.

"No!" I told myself. "You will NOT faint!"

I began breathing again, although it was heavy. The moment passed. I warded off passing out, afraid if I had, the airline would not let me get on the plane. At this point, my only objective was to get home.

Brock coaxed me into eating a few bites of rice and drinking a bottle of water.

"I think you may have exhaustion," he explained. "Is your mind fuzzy?"

"A little," I said.

He helped me get onto our last flight. I slept on and off, waking to extreme stomach pain.

At one point, I looked out the window. Hot tears slid down my cheeks as I begged the Lord to end this misery. I did not know what was going on in my body but I had never felt so badly in my life, not even when I had bronchitis in college.

I thankfully crawled into my bed that night and slept soundly for ten hours.

The next morning, I felt like my normal self until after lunch. Piercing pain began to rip through my stomach. The fleeting moments of nausea and fainting episodes were gone, but the burning discomfort came on and off throughout the day.

Brock decided I had eaten too much greasy food like fried halibut and fried crab nuggets in Alaska, and it had thrown off my body. He put me on a strict diet of grilled turkey or fish and lots of green vegetables. I began to feel a little better but still had that nagging stomach pain every afternoon and evening for the next few weeks.

****

It was April 5, 2006, and I was giddy with excitement as we sat in our dressing room backstage at the Grand Ole Opry for the televised *Gospel Music Awards*. It was like the Grammy's for Christian artists.

Brock was asked to present an award. We felt especially honored since usually Christian musicians were the ones asked to do this.

"I just met Vince Gill!" Brock said. "And my dressing room is next to Michael Sweet!"

"Kirk Franklin just complimented me on my dress!" I interjected, looking down at the pastel sleeveless dress with cream colored lace I had purchased at a store in California the week before. "This is like a dream."

"I know! I feel like we are on top of the world right now. I just did a TV special, we have gone to almost all of the states like you wanted, and now I'm presenting an award at the GMA's!"

I popped one of the artisan truffles specially made for the GMA's in my mouth. My stomach still didn't quite feel right, but I was feeling much better than I had been recently. I pushed it out of my mind and decided not to think about my physical issues that had been happening since we got back from Alaska. I wasn't going to let anything bring me down this night.

We heard a knock on the door and a young man wearing a headset poked his head inside. He informed us it was time to go onstage.

He handed Brock an envelope that read "Artist of the Year." As we walked to the stage, Brock asked the guy, "Am I presenting the Artist of the Year award?"

"Yes," the man answered in a matter-of-fact fashion.

"Isn't that the biggest award of the night?" I asked Brock.

"Yes!" He answered as we approached the stage.

I handed Brock his props and he proceeded onto the stage with Shirley Caesar. She was a legend in gospel music.

After Shirley listed all the candidates, Brock held up an envelope and said, "The award goes to..."

Suddenly, the envelope burst into flames and disintegrated into the air. Shirley Caesar saw the fire, screamed, and ran a few feet away from Brock.

"Come back here," he called to her. "I have a backup plan."

He then picked up a thin black briefcase and put it on a table. He opened the case to reveal a ten-pound bowling ball.

"Ooooh!" Shirley Caesar exclaimed. "How did that fit in there?"

Brock smiled and said, "There's something on the ball."

He flipped over the bowling ball and took off an envelope taped to it. He purposely dropped the ball on the stage.

Everyone present heard the loud thud and watched it roll away.

"Stay!" Brock said and the ball came to a halt.

The crowd laughed and clapped at the scene. After the applause died down, Brock said, "The winner of Artist of the Year is Chris Tomlin!"

From just behind the curtain, I leaped excitedly at the news. We had known Chris and his band for awhile. I thought about the youth camp in a small Texas town where we met him several years earlier. We exchanged stories from the road.

Two women dressed in evening gowns went out and handed Chris and his band members a golden trophy shaped like a dove.

I watched as Brock picked up the bowling ball and handed it to Chris's guitar player, Jesse. He was a practical joker, so Brock decided to play one on him.

When they all walked offstage, Jesse laughingly said to Brock. "I didn't know what to do with that bowling ball! I couldn't hold it and the award. It was awkward. I finally sat the ball on the ground."

Ben, one of the other band members, patted Brock on the back and said, "Good one, Brock!"

"Congratulations," Brock said to Chris.

"We never would have thought we'd be here when we sat at that camp in Texas so many years ago did we?" Chris said. "God has blessed us, you and me."

Before Brock could say anything, we were whisked into a press room for pictures and interviews.

Chris Tomlin and his band displayed their Dove awards as cameras flashed from all over the room. When it was Brock's turn to get his picture taken, he held the bowling ball up near his chest. In place of an award, Brock proudly sported a blue, shiny bowling ball. I laughed at the very characteristic Brock move.

Brock worked his way around the press room. As we were waiting for him to be interviewed by a Christian television program, he leaned down and said, "In all the commotion, I forgot to ask what the doctor said today."

All of the excitement from the night dissipated as the words of the doctor from earlier came floating back. "In order to get your body back on track, you are going to need to make some serious changes in your lifestyle. Otherwise, you will continue to have these stomach issues or even worse," she explained.

I forced a smile and said, "We can talk about it tomorrow. They are ready for you." I nodded toward a cameraman heading Brock's direction. I did not want to ruin Brock's night with the foreboding conversation I had with the doctor.

"Okay." Brock winked at me as he got ready to do his next interview.

As we packed up and headed home, Brock talked excitedly about the night. I intentionally made cheerful interjections. However, the entire time, I only had one thought going through my head. The only way to be healthy was to quit working and traveling so hard.

Was this the end of my days doing this ministry?

CHAPTER ELEVEN
Stormy Time

"God is our refuge and strength, an ever-present help in trouble. Therefore we will not fear, though the earth give way and the mountains fall into the heart of the sea, though its waters roar and foam and the mountains quake with their surging." Psalm 46:1-3

I woke up early the next morning. Glancing over at Brock sleeping soundly, I guessed I had two hours before he woke.

I poured myself a glass of water and fixed my usual breakfast of late, a bowl of granola and walnuts, drizzled with honey and topped with blueberries.

Bringing my bowl into the living room, I sat on the couch and cried out to God.

How could I change my lifestyle? This is what I was called to do when God told me as a young girl I would "marry someone in the ministry and be very involved."

When we performed a show and people responded to the gospel of Jesus, I felt invigorated, like I was created to do this. How could I quit? But that's the only alternative the doctor had given.

When she heard my typical show day schedule, she said I was working too much without a break. That, combined with a strenuous travel itinerary with different time zones and eating late at night were leading to acid reflux. She explained that acid was coming up from my stomach into my esophagus.

The doctor said I was in the beginning stages of this disease. If I didn't do something about it, I could have permanent damage.

After two hours of prayer, I felt as if the Lord gave me a solution. Now I needed to talk it over with Brock.

An hour later, I sat Brock down at the kitchen table and handed him a bowl of granola. Sitting across from him, I said, "I think we need to make some changes."

"What do you mean?" he asked, confused.

I explained what the doctor had told me. I could see Brock's eyes get wide. A look of panic formed in his expression, a stark contrast to his normally calm demeanor.

"Before you get upset," I said holding up my hand in protest. "I feel like God has given me an idea."

Brock pushed his food away and leaned forward in anticipation.

"Instead of doing our big illusion show everywhere we go, we do our fly show. This way we could fly to places like Houston instead of driving 16 hours one way. This would allow us to be home more."

Brock sat back in his chair and put his chin in his hand pensively.

"Also, my set up time would be cut a lot. I can pack up the show in 15 minutes without the assistance of any volunteers. Then, we would naturally eat dinner earlier because we would be done loading out earlier," I said trying to sound persuasive.

When Brock said nothing, I continued. "I know it wouldn't be as big a show as we have now, but our fly shows are more interactive. You use more audience members onstage and it portrays your personality more."

While the grand illusions where Brock cut me in half or made me disappear were impressive, they were similar to many other illusionists and were done to music. Brock excelled when he did things that showed off his daring personality like escapes and stunts or his quick wit like teasing a volunteer onstage while he performed an original card trick.

He looked at me and smiled. "I have a better idea."

He then began to explain that he had been working on a new stunt. In this effect, there would be a blue and red tube on opposite sides of the stage. A ten foot ladder would be next to each tube. He would bring one girl from the audience onstage and allow her to choose which tube Brock would use. After she made her decision, he would climb the ladder next to the corresponding tube of her choice and jump down smashing it. He would then lift the remaining tube revealing a large sword under it.

"I even know exactly how to use this as an illustration for the gospel. I could talk about choices and how some lead to life and death. Jesus is the ultimate choice that leads to eternal life. What do you think?" he asked.

"I like the idea, but how can we fly with it?"

"We can check the sword and some kind of stand to hold it upright in a hardshell case. We can request the promotor provide the ladders and blue and red poster board. I can make the tubes when I get there."

"So we can do a show that packs small but plays big," I said becoming more hopeful.

"Exactly," Brock said nodding. "Plus, it will take little time to set up and tear down."

We immediately began putting together a new show. We also decided to make some dietary changes.

In the following months, we took granola, walnuts, and honey with us so we could have a consistent breakfast everyday. On show days, we made sure to eat a large, healthy lunch. For dinner, we had the host provide grilled chicken or fish and vegetables at the venue 30 minutes after our show. This ensured we could eat right away instead of having to sit down and order food at the restaurant.

****

Two months later, I ran out the back door of the convention center in Jekyll Island, Georgia and into the bright sunshine. We were performing and speaking at youth conferences there for three weeks in a row.

That morning, we performed the routine with the ladders in the youth convention service and it went perfectly. I felt exhilarated by the potential of our new show!

"Let's get some lunch," Brock said. As we headed toward the parking lot, his phone rang and he answered.

Shortly into the call, he stopped walking. His expression grew dim. "It's Todd," he mouthed to me, referring to the youth pastor at our church when we lived in Houston.

After we moved, Todd changed careers from being a pastor to being a house contractor. He financed and managed the building of new houses. Then, he'd sell each house and make a nice profit. For the last few years, his business had been booming.

When he asked if we wanted to partner with him on one house and make some money a couple of years before, we agreed. After seeing the trials we had gone through financially like the trailer theft and truck fire, he wanted to help us get more stable monetarily.

It seemed like an easy investment. We put the loan for the new house in our name, but Todd paid the mortgage. When Todd sold the house, we would receive some money.

When Brock said goodbye, he sat down on the steps leading to the parking lot. I looked at him and asked what was wrong.

"Apparently, Todd has had some financial problems and has not paid the mortgage on the house we invested in for several months. It's in danger of being foreclosed."

"What?" I asked. "When is the foreclosing?"

"Next week," Brock answered sounding defeated.

"How much do we need to get us out of this mess?"

"Twenty-thousand dollars in back mortgage or one hundred seventy-thousand dollars to purchase the house."

"We don't have that kind of money! Call Todd back and tell him he needs to do something!"

"Auny, it won't do any good to call him. He cannot do anything about it."

"Why our house? Why not any of the others?"

"All of the houses he owns right now are not selling. We are not the only ones whose house is foreclosing."

"Well, I am going to call him and let him know that he needs to fix this!"

I reached down and pulled out my phone to dial his number and it instantly began ringing. It was my mom.

When I answered, she immediately knew something was wrong. In hearing her familiar voice, emotion overcame me. I tearfully explained what was going on. I filled her in even up to the point in which I was about to call Todd when she called me.

Mom gently said, "I don't think it's a good idea to call him. You don't want to be responsible for what that man might do to himself if you turn on him. I'm sure plenty of others have. Even if this does end badly, you need to be the one to forgive him."

Her words sunk deep into my heart. I was getting so wrapped up in what I thought would happen to us that I had not even considered what was happening to Todd. His business was drying up. He had no money. He had a wife and five children to provide for.

I looked over at Brock who was now talking with someone on his phone to try and figure something out. His voice was not raised in anger now or when he was on the phone with Todd.

From that moment on, I supported my patient husband.

For the next week, we performed and spoke onstage and God was moving, and we painted a smile on our faces. However, on the inside, we were in turmoil, because we were watching our financial security fall apart.

After we finished each show, we would get on the phone or online and research how we could avoid a foreclosure. We enlisted many smart people to give us advice, but every one of them said the same thing. If we didn't sell the house, it would foreclose.

We set some things in motion that would postpone the foreclosure and buy us more time. We were praying the postponement would come through on the day of the foreclosure. We were down to the wire. It did not, and the foreclosure was still on schedule.

On the dreaded day, I looked out of our hotel onto the beautiful Jekyll Island beach. The sun glistened off the water. Surely the Lord who made this vast ocean could work out a little thing like this.

I felt the water drawing me out. "I'm going to take a walk," I mouthed to Brock since he was on the phone with yet another financial guy.

As the salty breeze filled my senses, I realized I had not been out on the beach at all this week. We had been cooped up in our room trying to dodge the bullet of our financial ruin.

Today was the day. It would be over with, one way or another. That certainty was comforting as I walked down the steps and onto the sand.

Walking parallel to the water, I began pleading again and again for the Lord would step in and give us a miracle. "You can be my night in shining armor like You've done so many times before," I told Him.

I began to weep. "Lord, it feels like things are going so well! We have more shows on the books than ever before. We have community at home. I'm afraid this one bad investment might take it all away! What if we have to go bankrupt? What if we lose our house in Nashville? Lord, please give us a miracle! Give us the money to buy the house. If the money came in right now, You would be stepping in at the last hour and saving the day!"

Then, I heard the whisper of the Lord. "Not this time," was what He said.

I stopped walking and watched the waves beating the shore. All of the fight left me. I breathed in a deep breath.

As I did, something began to spread down through my body. I was overcome by an unexplainable peace.

A scripture in Romans chapter five came into my mind. "We know that suffering produces perseverance, perseverance character, and character hope."

No matter what happened from this point on, I had hope because I had the Lord. Even if He did not provide the funds to pay for the house, He would still be there for me.

I began to actually smile. I wiggled my feet and felt the sand between my toes. This was not the end of the world. The Lord had seen us through trials before. He would see us through this as well.

The house foreclosed that day ruining our excellent credit. What would this mean for our future? Would we go bankrupt?

How would this affect our ministry?

CHAPTER TWELVE
A Divine Meeting

"No eye has seen, no ear has heard, no mind has conceived what God has prepared for those who love Him." II Corinthians 2:9

A few weeks later, Brock's phone rang and he mouthed that it was our financial business advisor. This is the call we had been waiting to receive. We would finally learn how much damage the foreclosure would bring.

I walked out on the back porch of our house in order to give Brock privacy. I looked out at the grassy hill speckled with various sized trees.

Gazing up into the bright, blue sky, I prayed. "Lord, we need your help. I know You own cattle on a thousand hills. We just need You to help us with our little hill here. Please, don't let us lose this house. Don't let us go bankrupt. We need You."

A few minutes later, Brock joined me on the porch. "Well, time will tell, but it's not as bad as I expected."

He went on to explain that our credit would not be good for a while. Therefore, we probably couldn't take out a loan any time within the next seven years. Other than that, our lives would not change. The housing market was crashing and many were in the same predicament as we.

"So, we just have to pray we don't need to take out any loans in the next seven years?" I asked.

"Yes, and we need to live in this house for a long time." He said as he came up behind me and put his arms around me.

"I can do that. I like this house." I said breathing in a sigh of relief.

After discussing it with Brock for a while, I went inside and sat on the couch. I opened our laptop and wrote a blog entry.

I had been blogging every day for the last year. It was therapeutic to write out the occurrences we were experiencing with God and on the road. Plus, it felt good to share them with others. It also helped to have some know exactly what we needed prayers for at the time.

I had some faithful readers who commented regularly. I knew some of them personally but others had seen us at a show or on television.

My favorite commenter was Barbara. She had seen *The Miracles of Jesus* and then found Brock and my blogs online. Barbara lived in Salteo, Mexico, a small town outside of Monterey.

The language barrier made some of her comments comical. Instead of saying, "I laughed so hard, I almost peed," she said, "There is pee in my belly as I laugh."

I finished filling my blog audience in on what was happening with us financially. Then, I picked up my Bible which was laying on the end table.

Flipping to the back, I looked at the picture I had taped to the back cover. In the picture was an empty wooden chair sitting on the end of a pier jetting out over the ocean. Two sandals sat at the base of the chair. The caption read, "'Be still and know that I am God.' Psalm 46:10."

Peace wrapped itself around me as I meditated on these simple words. I thought about how difficult it was for me to be still. I was a doer and wanted to make things happen. In this foreclosure fiasco, there was nothing I could do. I had to trust God would take care of us.

I rubbed the leather cover and the words the Lord had spoken to me a few months before during my routine Bible study time came back to me. "I want you to give your Bible to someone," was what He said. When I asked who and when, I didn't receive any answers.

Since that day in April, I met a few good candidates to receive my

Bible. Some girls from a girls' home came to our show in North Carolina and a few of them gave their lives to Christ. I asked the Lord if one of them was the one He had in mind. He gently told me "No."

When we met Deion, a kid from the inner city of Atlanta, I was certain he was the one. He attended a student conference where Brock spoke about what he had discovered while filming *The Miracles of Jesus*. Brock explained that he had reenacted some of the miracles by using slight of hand and modern technology. He was more convinced now than ever before that Jesus was the real thing. He performed actual miracles.

After the service, twelve year old Deion came running up to Brock. He asked him to fix his teeth. He said he got made fun of because of his jagged smile but did not have the money to go to a dentist. He wanted Brock to supernaturally fix his teeth.

Brock patiently told Deion what he does onstage with his illusions is not supernatural. After he spoke with him for a while, we found some leaders from his church. They found a dentist in the area and planned to take Deion to him as soon as they got home.

I went to grab my Bible out of my backpack to give it to Deion. As I reached in and grabbed it, I had a feeling it was not right.

Everyday, I prayed for the person the Lord intended for me to give my Bible to. I prayed for his or her heart to be drawn to God.

****

Over a year later, we were doing a show in Houston, Texas. Before the show began, someone said there was a girl all the way from Mexico here to see us. I knew it could only be one person...Barbara, my favorite commenter on my blog.

I never thought I would get to meet Barbara face-to-face, but apparently she was here. I began to search for her. I ran out into the lobby and there she was. She was a beautiful twenty year old girl with long, dark curly hair and fair skin. She was timidly looking down to the floor.

"Barbara!" I yelled to her.

Her eyes met mine and there was an instant connection between us. I felt like she was so familiar to me, like family, even though this was our first meeting.

She seemed vulnerable and young standing alone in the lobby of the church. I ran to her and wrapped her in a hug.

My first question was, "How did you get here?"

"I road the bus," she replied shyly.

"Was that a long bus ride?" I asked.

"Only 30 hours," she said with a snicker.

We both laughed, and I took her to the stage to meet Brock. Brock was shocked, and I could tell by the look on his face that he felt that same connection to her as I did.

"Barbara spent 30 hours on a bus to get here!" I told Brock.

"Bus was easy. Getting to church was hard," Barbara said.

Then, she explained in her broken English that all she had to go by was a piece of paper with the address of the church on it. So, she showed it to a cab driver at the bus station. He dropped her off at the front entrance of the church. However, this church was huge and had several buildings. We happened to be in the building in the back. She walked around the whole church property before finding us.

Barbara sat on the front row when the show began. I kept peeking out at her from behind the curtain. I did not know how much she would understand. She seemed to be speaking great English, but I had not spent enough time with her to know how much she could grasp.

I watched as she laughed and then she began to cry a little. When Brock gave everyone the opportunity to give their lives to Christ, I was amazed when Barbara was one of the first ones to stand up saying she was ready to follow Jesus.

After the show, we asked Barbara her plans. She really did not have any. Her only goal was to see Brock's show. We took her to dinner and got her a room at the hotel where we were staying that night.

At dinner, Brock asked her, "How did you learn English? You are speaking so well!"

Barbara began to tell us her story. She had always wanted to learn English. One day, she was flipping through the channels and came across Brock on the Discovery Channel on the show he hosted, *The Miracles of Jesus*. She thought that Brock had a clear voice.

With Spanish subtitles, she was able to read what Brock was saying in English. After watching the whole three-hour special on the miracles of Jesus, she was not only drawn to Brock, but to Jesus.

She found Brock's blog online and began reading it. She said it took her hours to read one paragraph at first using an online translator. Each day, she became better and better at it. She eventually began reading my blog as well.

"Wait a second," Brock interrupted her. "You are telling me you learned English by reading my blog?"

Barbara smiled and said, "Yes."

We fell in love with Barbara. She had a timid yet determined way about her. Conversation came easily that night. It felt as if we were talking to a long lost friend or cousin.

The next morning I woke early in order to get ready. Brock was speaking during two services at the church.

I sat up in bed and placed my feet on the floor. Before, I stood up, I heard the Lord's voice clearly. "Barbara is the one I want you to give your Bible to."

I excitedly said, "Really? She's the one I've been praying for all this time?"

I felt confirmation in my heart.

Barbara went with us to the church. After the services, we took her and some of the people from the church to lunch with us.

One of the church leaders said, "We are actually going to Mexico next week on a mission trip."

Barbara asked, "Where are you going?"

"Salteo, outside of Monterey," he answered.

"That's where I am from!" Barbara excitedly exclaimed. "Where exactly in Salteo are you going to be?"

They explained where they would be and Barbara's jaw dropped. "That's two blocks from my house!"

"Well," the youth pastor said, "we need another interpreter. Do you think you could help us?"

"I'd love to!" Barbara said with no hesitation.

We laughed and took a lot of pictures while at lunch, but I could tell our time with Barbara was coming to an end. We had to go the next city to do another show and someone from the church was going to drive Barbara to the bus station.

I pulled Barbara aside and told her I had a gift for her. She looked at me with anticipation.

I handed her my Bible...the one with all my personal markings on it. I showed her where the gospels were so she could read more about Jesus herself.

With tears in her eyes, Barbara accepted the Bible.

"Barbara, the Lord told me He wanted me to give this Bible to someone last April. I don't know why He told me so long ago."

"I know why," she said tears glistening in her eyes.

"Last April was when I was watched *The Miracles of Jesus*. It was the first time I heard anything about Brock Gill," she said as she clutched the Bible with both hands.

I began to cry and I hugged Barbara.

"I have been praying for you ever since that day. I didn't know it was you I was praying for, but I did it nonetheless." I whispered in her ear.

After I released her, I said. "The Lord was letting me know there was a special girl out there."

A few minutes later, we talked about Barbara coming to stay with us sometime the following year. Then, we sadly said goodbye.

"I will keep in touch," she said as she got into the church member's car.

"You better!" Brock said.

We watched her ride away knowing this was the beginning of a wonderful friendship.

Barbara inspired us to want to reach out to people in other countries. We soon joined a group called Compassion International. This organization exposed us to more adventures in foreign places.

CHAPTER THIRTEEN
Parties with a Purpose

"Each man should give what he has decided in his heart to give, not reluctantly or under compulsion, for God loves a cheerful giver."
II Corinthians 9:7

"They are going to be here any minute!" I said excitedly at noon on Thanksgiving Day, 2007. Ryan, a BMX rider in his mid twenties who had performed with us at the Freedom Experience, helped me put the rolls in the oven.

He had been living with us for the last few months. After his grandma passed away, he had nowhere to go. We persuaded him to move from Minneapolis to our house.

The night Ryan moved in, I showed him the guest bedroom with an adjoining bathroom where he would be staying. He said, "I've never had this before."

"What? Your own bedroom?" I asked.

"No, a bed." He had slept on couches at friends' and families' houses his whole life.

"How many are coming today?" Ryan asked, breaking into my thoughts.

I quickly calculated in my head. "I think there will be about 30 of us."

"Whoa! That's a lot!" He replied.

"Well, Group 1 Crew is in town working on their album, so they are coming and a couple of the Eleventyseven guys will be here too," I said referring to the Christian bands who participated in the Freedom Experience with us. "The rest are some single people we know who either don't have families to go home to or have to work tomorrow and cannot drive home."

I smiled as I thought of the single people the Lord had brought into our lives over the last few years. They were about five to ten years younger than we. Many of them came from broken homes. All of them didn't have family in town.

Since our families lived in Louisiana and Texas, distance being an issue, we invited friends over for many holidays. Brock and I enjoyed hosting and cooking.

The doorbell rang and I welcomed the first of many guests. After eating turkey and dressing along with a plethora of side dishes and desserts, the group took a walk down the rural road where we live.

Then, we watched a movie. People were spread out all over the living room. I glanced around and looked at our beautiful, talented friends.

The amount of love and hope for their future I felt was supernatural. We were not family by blood, but through God, we were family.

"Having a good time?" Brock whispered from his seat next to me on the couch.

"It's been wonderful," I responded with a content sigh.

"Some have told me it was the best Thanksgiving they've ever had," Brock said.

It broke my heart to think about some of them not having a healthy family situation on Thanksgiving. Their holidays were often filled with friction or loneliness.

"I think everyone said your turkey was the best they've ever had," I said smiling up at Brock.

"That's because they've never had one cooked in a Cajun microwave before," he commented referring to his unique box cooker made by his uncle from Louisiana. He smoked the turkey in it for twelve hours making it tender and juicy.

I lay my head on Brock's shoulder and drifted off to sleep.

****

Through some of our friends in the Christian music industry, we were introduced to a nonprofit organization called Compassion International. This organization enlisted sponsors in the United States to pay monthly to support children all over the world. These children received a good meal everyday, extended education, medical services, and the message of the gospel.

The following January, Brock and I went to Guayaquil, Ecuador to visit one of the Compassion projects.

We went into their little building in the city where the children involved in the program came everyday after school.

I was impressed that we were the only Americans there. All of the workers at Compassion were locals. I was so uplifted by the ministry of this mission. They were breaking the poverty cycle as well as spreading the love and good news of Jesus throughout their community.

We shared a meal with the workers and children. Then, Brock performed a few illusions for them.

After the show, I gathered the children around Brock to take a picture. The boys close to Brock kept touching his goatee. They were fascinated by his facial hair.

Brock said, "Everyone say, 'Queso!'" knowing it did not have the same effect as "cheese." I laughed as the picture came out looking like everyone was singing since they were making an "o" shape with their mouths.

When I began to giggle, they began to as well. I then snapped a picture of everyone laughing.

After visiting the center, we went to the house of one of the children involved in Compassion. We pulled up to an area which looked like several abandoned warehouses. I looked around at the dilapidated buildings and thought, "Surely nobody lives here."

That's when I saw it. Little heads began popping up from holes in the structures. Children timidly poked their faces out at us. I smiled at one little boy. He smiled and quickly ran away.

Our guide from Compassion went up to the building that looked the most condemned. She knocked on the door (which I did not think was a door...it was more like a wall).

After we were let in, we were guided through a building with a roof that was caving in and no back wall to the building. Behind it was something similar to a trailer house. The only difference was it was one big room with partially straw walls. There were doorways and holes where windows would be but no glass or doors. They were all open to bugs and rain.

The mother greeted us at the door. Through the interpreter, she proudly said, "Welcome to our new home."

I looked around the place and it was definitely clean. You could practically eat off the floor. There was one big bed in the back corner and a small table with some chairs. However, there was no kitchen or bathroom that I could see. But from the look on the mom's face, it was a million-dollar home.

We sat in one of the chairs as the mother introduced us to her two beautiful daughters, Genesis and Emily. As the girls sang and danced for us, my heart melted.

With the help of a translator, Brock asked Genesis, who was ten years old, what she wanted to be when she grew up. Genesis said she wanted to be a veterinarian.

"Yes," the mom said. "Genesis loves animals! One time, she begged me to buy her a parrot. A parrot costs five dollars and that is more than we can afford. So, I told her to pray God would give her a parrot. Genesis began to pray for a parrot."

"A few days later," the mom continued, "Emily was shouting that there was a parrot on the roof. We put some bread out for the parrot and it came in. It's been our pet ever since."

At that moment while the mother was telling the story, Genesis left the room and came back with a parrot. The parrot had no cage, but it stayed right there at their house! The faith of this family living in this small little place which would be condemned in the United States inspired me to the core.

As the girls showed us the parrot, the mother said, "Now, we are praying in faith that our house will get paid off so we can put effort into rebuilding my husband's garage so he can work as a mechanic again."

"If you don't mind me asking, how much do you owe on your house?" Brock said.

"We owe $450 and our mortgage is $13 a month," she responded.

I let that sink in for a minute. In Ecuador, they used the American dollar, so it was dollar for dollar. She paid the same amount of money for her house note that we had just spent on lunch!

Brock gave me a telling look. I knew he had set his mind on buying this family the house.

We felt so blessed to have a house. Could we provide one for this family a continent away? She seemed to have the same open door policy we had. I began praying we would get the money in order to be able to help this family.

I tearfully hugged the mom and two girls as we left to go back to our hotel.

****

Before we flew back home, we purchased some rare Ecuadorian chocolate. We love chocolate and they grow cacao trees in Ecuador.

A plan began forming in Brock's head. He decided we would have a chocolate tasting to raise money to pay off this family's house.

When we got home, we planned a big party at our house. On Valentine's Day, we had a great dinner and then tasted some chocolate we brought home from Ecuador.

As Brock began telling the story about the family we met on our trip, I began to get worried. I looked around at all the single people without a support system from their family. Many of them were starving artists trying to make it in the Christian music industry.

"These people cannot afford to give anything," I thought. "They barely have enough money to get by."

"Normally, you all come over here and eat for free which is fine with us." Brock was telling our guests. "However, if you would had eaten out tonight, you probably would have spent $10 or so. I am asking you to give that $10 to this family in Ecuador. All of us here are going to buy them a house!"

I could see some people's eyes light up. "This could really work!" I thought.

We raised $750 for the Ecuadorian family. They were able to pay off their house and begin working on the garage.

Everyone loved being able to help someone in need so much that they asked when we were going to do it again. We decided that we'd do it the next month, too, only we would find another need.

That Easter, we collected 78 pairs of shoes for a ministry called Soles 4 Souls. They provided people in third world countries shoes.

As we were praying about who to raise money for in the month of May, Brock called our friend, Travis, who had uprooted his family and moved from Alabama to Hollywood because he had a heart to reach people in the movie industry. Brock asked him how things were going.

Travis said it was going well and his wife was pregnant. This was a big surprise! They had two older daughters who were eleven and eight. They thought they were done with baby things. To add to the scenario, this baby was going to be a boy. Travis explained that living in Los Angeles was quite expensive and money was tight.

Brock told him our community was looking for someone to give to. He said we wanted to throw them a baby shower through the internet sometime in May.

Travis couldn't believe it! That's when his wife was due. Plus, they didn't have the support system they had in place in Alabama, so nobody was planning on throwing them a baby shower even though they really needed it.

When I found out that we were going to be throwing a baby shower, I laughed to myself. We lived in Nashville, so most everyone who came to our parties were artsy. In our group, we had a rocker chic, motocross racer, freestyle BMX rider, fire eater, tattoo artist, and us. We weren't exactly the crowd to give a baby shower.

However, on Mother's Day, we did just that. I snickered at the sight of three guys with tattoo-covered arms sitting at our dining room table perusing baby stuff on their computers.

Ryan looked up at me and said, "I purchased them a baby gate. That way the baby won't fall down the stairs."

"You do backflips on your bicycle. I never pegged you as safety conscience," I answered.

"Auny, we are talking about a baby here. Plus, it's on their registry," he said pointing to the picture of the gate on his laptop screen.

"I think it's a great gift," I said smiling.

Not a person in the group had a child, but they were willing to help. It warmed my heart.

We named our new ministry endeavor "Parties with a Purpose."

Over the next year, we had one of these parties at our house every month.

We raised money for missionaries in Brazil and Africa and an orphanage in Haiti which had been hit with three hurricanes. We gave to an organization who rescued child soldiers in Burma.

Between the "Parties with a Purpose," we continued performing shows across the country. At the end of every show, Brock spoke about Compassion International. We began to acquire sponsors for hundreds of children all over the world. The more sponsors, the more children got to hear the hope of Jesus Christ.

Through Parties with a Purpose and Compassion International, our ministry extended outside of the United States and into foreign countries.

Little did I know that the most terrifying moment of my life would take place in one of these foreign countries.

CHAPTER FOURTEEN
Dreams and Nightmares

"For God does speak—now one way, now another—though man may not perceive it. In a dream, in a vision of the night, when deep sleep falls on men as they slumber in their beds, He may speak in their ears and terrify them with warnings." Job 33:14-16

Brock and I had just left a venue where we performed. We were exiting the building out into the city. As I walked along the sidewalk, I stepped over something lying on the ground. I quickly turned around to inspect what I almost stepped on. There was a large, ugly snake hissing at me. It had a triangular head, which I remember from watching Animal Planet, means it was venomous. The way in which the snake's head hung up in the air made me think it was a cobra. Its vicious eyes bored into mine. I looked at Brock hoping he could save me, but now the snake was in between Brock and me.

Just then, Brock picked up a rock and threw it at the snake trying to get the vile cobra's attention off of me. It seemed like a good plan, but it backfired. The snake began slithering after me. I took off in a full-on sprint!

I ran down the sidewalk knowing the snake was on my heels. I pictured it lashing out and sinking its fangs into my calves.

After turning the corner, I glanced to see if the snake was still behind me. When I discovered it was not, I breathed a sigh of relief and stopped running.

When I looked in front of me, I gasped overtaken with fear. In the tree and on the ground surrounding me were snakes too numerous to count. They were draped along the branches and in the scrubs. I noticed every single one had a triangular head and looked just like the

155

cobra that had come after me.

At that moment, all of the snakes stopped slithering around and turned their big heads in my direction. They stared at me, looking me eye to eye, hissing and perched to attack.

The hairs on the back of my neck stood up and I froze. What should I do? There were too many snakes to escape!

I sat straight up in bed breathing very heavily! I looked around the hotel room and saw that no snakes were present and I was safe. My breath returned to a slower pace.

I tried to shake off the dream as I stepped into the shower. It felt so real. Usually, I can trace a dream back to something I watched or talked about the day before, but snakes had not been on my radar in as long as I could remember.

Later that morning, Brock said, "What's going on? You seem distracted."

I told him everything about my dream. I explained that this dream was different from any other I had ever had. Usually they were really fuzzy, but this one was detailed and clear.

"You want to know something weird?" Brock asked. "I had the same dream last night."

We thought this was unusual but we chalked it up to coincidence.

A couple of weeks later, we were sitting at the table on Thanksgiving Day, 2008, and Brock leaned over to me and said, "I had another dream about snakes last night."

An eerie feeling came over me as I responded with, "So did I. This time, the snake bit me."

"The snake bit me too," Brock said.

After our friends left and I was placing the last plate in the dishwasher, Brock came in the kitchen and leaned against the counter.

"Do you think God is telling us something through these dreams?" he asked pensively.

"In the Bible, He used dreams sometimes to communicate. I cannot believe it's a coincidence now, not after it's happened twice on the same night for us both," I answered.

"Well, snakes could represent so many things like danger, deception, or even Satan."

A knot began to form in my stomach. Of all the things snakes could mean, none of them were good.

"The dreams seem to cut off right when we are in trouble. So, if something is going to happen to us that's dangerous, I don't know how it will end?" I said as I pushed the button turning on the dishwasher.

Brock came and placed his arms around me resting his hands on the small of my back. "We need to pray about it and trust the Lord to deliver us."

"Yes, and I think we should ask someone else to pray with us."

"Who should we ask? It sounds very strange that we think we may be in danger because we had a dream about snakes."

"That's why we need to tell someone we trust. Someone who knows we aren't crazy."

"What about Rod and Susan?" Brock asked as he walked out of the kitchen and turned off the lights.

I followed him into the bedroom. I had prayed for Susan for several months on a simple message I heard the Lord say in my head, and it ended up being warranted. They had seen the power of prayer and would be the perfect ones to share this unusual occurrence with.

The next week, we told them about the dreams in detail. They agreed that the fact we had the same dream on the same night was significant. We all began to pray about what it meant, as well as protection from whatever was about to take place.

****

A few months went by as we continued to pray and be on guard. As I was driving through the city where we live, I noticed a big hawk sitting on a street sign a few feet from my car. Its wings were spread out very majestically. It was so close! "Wow," I whispered to the empty car, "that's magnificent!"

On the way home that day, another hawk swooped down in front of me almost hitting my windshield. In the next ten minutes, I saw two more hawks.

I had never encountered a hawk so close but to have four in one day was noteworthy. I felt as if the Lord was trying to get my attention.

When I got home, I quickly looked up "hawk" in the concordance of my Bible but found nothing. There were scriptures about eagles..."they shall mount up with wings like eagles." (Isaiah 40:30-31) But I specifically saw hawks.

I decided to turn to the internet to continue my research. There I found out hawks eat an average of two snakes every couple of days. I read an eyewitness account of a hawk swooping down and hovering over the ground with its wings spread. Then, it flew away with a snake in its talons.

Maybe the Lord was trying to show me that He was the glorious bird who could take care of a snake in a second! He could swoop down and save us.

I had not done my daily Bible study yet, so I pulled out the one I was currently reading. This study was teaching me how symbolic the Lord was. Every inch of His tabernacle had layers of meaning.

At the top of the page, there was a scripture verse listed. Chills ran down my spine as I read the verse for that day. "He will cover you with His feathers. Under His wings, you will find refuge." (Psalm 91:4)

I immediately dove into the study. I drank in every word, especially the scriptures. The rest of the study for that day dealt with verses in the

Bible about wings and feathers such as Psalm 17:8, "Keep me as the apple of Your eye; Hide me in the shadow of Your wings."

Reasoning began to set in. No wonder the Lord displayed hawks and not eagles in front of me. The scriptures about eagles pertained to strength, but the ones about wings dealt with protection.

I excitedly went to Brock and told him everything I had found pointing out the scriptures concerning God's protection.

"I feel like the message the Lord has given me is that as long as we stay in the shadow of His wing, He will protect us," I declared.

"That gives me hope," Brock replied.

We didn't know what kind of protection we needed, so we continued praying for protection all around. Brock felt as if he needed to pray for physical protection, so he did so very diligently.

****

The following summer, Brock had spoken at a few Christian youth conferences on the east coast and we had a couple of days to repack and get to Texas for another week-long conference. I could hear Brock on the phone in the living room as I placed clothes into an open suitcase lying on our bed.

My mind drifted back to a few days before when Brock shared with the students about losing a house in a business deal with a friend that went bad. He chose to forgive. He explained in simple terms that he could be bitter or better because of this unfortunate event. He powerfully conveyed that it is best to forgive, because through Jesus, God had forgiven us. We all deserve hell, but through God's miraculous grace we can be forgiven. Those of us who are Christians should forgive others, because we have been forgiven by God.

He then had the students have a time to pray and think about people they needed to forgive in their lives. Some went to their leaders to talk about how to forgive.

Tears came to my eyes as I heard many people throughout the audience crying. A few people went out into the hallway and got on the phone expressing forgiveness to whoever was on the other end of the receiver. I watched a big, high school guy go up to his pastor and bury his head in his chest as he shook with sobs. Some of the students present had been wronged more than I could imagine. It was only by the supernatural power of the Lord that they were able to forgive.

Brock entered the room, interrupting my thoughts. "You have to hear this story," he said, sitting on the edge of the bed.

He had been on the phone with the camp director of the previous camp. He explained that the day he spoke on forgiveness, one girl told her church leader she was forgiving her stepfather for molesting her. Her youth pastor decided he needed to do something about it. He contacted the authorities and when they got home from the event, a few police officers were waiting in his office at the church to take a statement from the girl.

The girl's mom and stepfather were in the parking lot of the church to pick up her and her sister. The youth pastor made up some excuse about getting the mom to sign something in order to get her into the office. When she got there, they told her what her daughter had said. She turned to her daughter and said, "Now, you have said this once before but then you recanted. Is it the truth?" She looked at her daughter doubtfully when her other daughter spoke up and said, "He's been doing it to me too."

That poor mom lost it! She became furious and was about to go out to confront her husband. It took all *three* police officers to restrain her.

The youth pastor went out to the car to calmly get the stepfather to come inside. The stepfather had moved from the passenger's seat to the driver's seat. Before the pastor could get to him, he peeled out of the church parking lot. He knew he had been found out.

When the youth pastor came back inside, the girls sat their mother down and told her that she needed to forgive him just like Jesus had forgiven her. They explained that is what they had learned to do at the conference where they had heard Brock speak, and there is freedom in forgiveness.

I began to get emotional as Brock finished the story. "Only through God's strength could anybody forgive that man," I said quietly.

"It puts perspective on what happened to us. So we defaulted on a house. So what?" Brock said with a laugh void of humor.

"You're absolutely right. However, look how your testimony is affecting others. You didn't hesitate to forgive, Brock. If you didn't choose to forgive, you wouldn't be sharing this story. Also, if it didn't happen, you would have no story to share."

"I think all forgiveness is from the Lord. It's not natural to forgive. Our flesh wants to hold onto the self pity and bitterness."

"You're right again," I said closing up the suitcase. "I'm ready to go."

On our flight to Texas, my thoughts kept going back to those girls who had learned at a very young age the power in forgiveness. I prayed for the girls and that their mother would handle this horrible situation as maturely as her daughters had.

****

The student convention was going well, but we were quite drained since this was our sixth week-long conference of the summer. On the third day, I went to the bathroom as the morning service dismissed and the majority of the attendees congregated in the hallway.

Looking in the mirror, I sighed. That morning, as I was eating breakfast in the lobby of the hotel where we were staying, a kind elderly lady who worked the buffet approached me. She sweetly asked, "Can I get you anything else?"

The thought entered my mind, "You can leave me alone!"

As quickly as the thought came up, I pushed it down and smiled. "No, thank you," I responded.

"You have a good day now," the woman said as she left my table to tend to others sitting around me.

I felt at any minute I could snap! Being on the road for the last two months without much down time had left me at a breaking point.

On the road, you get pushed to your limits often. No routine, lots of travel, not much sleep, working with people you just met, and being "on" much of the time is a recipe for a blow up.

I had a rule I went by. If every person around me was annoying me, it was not them, it was me. I was the one who had a problem. When I got like this, I knew I needed to take it easy and if at all possible, spend some time alone. This was such a day.

At that moment, Rosa entered the restroom. "Hi," she said as she approached me.

Rosa was a security guard at the venue where we had the camp services. From the first day, I felt drawn to her, as if the Lord wanted me to befriend her. Every morning, I'd see Rosa and go and speak with her. She was from Mexico and didn't speak perfect English, but we were still able to communicate.

I smiled at her wearily and said hi.

She came up to me and took my hands in hers. She tearfully said, "You and your husband are warriors for my Lord. Thank you for speaking to these kids. Keep following your heart and always listen to His voice." Her eyes were so kind and genuine that I felt like I was looking into the eyes of Jesus.

I pulled her into an embrace. I thought the Lord wanted me to befriend Rosa for her benefit, but I was beginning to think it was for mine. In a few words, she had uplifted me.

When I went back into the hall, Brock was the only one left. "There you are!" he exclaimed. "I think we need to get away for a little while this afternoon."

I agreed and we decided to take a day trip over to Matamoros, Mexico since it was close to where we were. Brock and I had both been there years before and it was a great place to shop and eat in the touristy market.

We parked our rental car on the Texas side. As we parked, some guys asked Brock if he was Kid Rock. I thought, "So much for not sticking out."

Not only was Brock 6'4" tall, but he also had long blonde hair and blue eyes. He was obviously American.

We walked across the border and over a big bridge. When we got on the Mexican side, we caught a taxi to the market. That's where the shops and restaurants were located.

"I can't wait to eat authentic Mexican food. Remember those tacos we had when we were in Mexico on our honeymoon?" I asked Brock.

"Those were the best! I'm so ready for lunch," he said as the cab slowed and pulled into a parking lot near a warehouse.

A knot began forming in the pit of my stomach. This was not the market. I pictured men barging out of the warehouse and snatching us out of the cab at gun point.

The driver was saying something about waiting for us and charging us for the whole day. My nerves eased a little when I thought the cab driver was simply trying to get more money out of us. Because of the language barrier, I was not completely clear about what he was saying. One thing was certain. This place gave me the creeps.

"Let's get out of here," I whispered to Brock.

"Where's the market?" Brock asked the taxi driver.

He pointed and said it was a couple of blocks away. He was still pleading with us to let him escort us as Brock paid him for the fare, and we ran off in the direction which he indicated.

We rounded the corner into the market, and I immediately felt uneasy. This was not like the time I had come years before. No children roamed the streets selling Chiclets. There were not any tourists.

Shops with blankets and hammocks and such lined the sidewalk. However, nobody seemed to be shopping. There were a dozen people congregated around a table.

"They are playing three card monte only they are using three shells and a pea," Brock whispered to me.

We were familiar with three card monte. It's a magic trick which Brock was able to do but never did since he was too honest. It's a swindle using three cards, two the same and one queen. The card handler shows you the three cards and then turns them face down and switches them around. Then, he bets you cannot find the queen. No matter which one you point to, the magician makes sure you do not find the queen, taking all of your money.

In the streets of Mexico, they were using three shells and a pea. You had to find the pea. Since Brock knew how the con worked, he told me not to make eye contact with anyone at the tables.

"This is so interesting to me how they are using this magic trick to swindle people out of money," Brock whispered.

We walked further down the sidewalk and found two more tables of people playing three card monte with the shells and pea.

"I'd like to get this on film," Brock said. He stood several feet away from the table, but there was a clear view of it behind him.

"Act like you are taking a picture of me, but really video the table behind me," he instructed.

I did what he said. A few seconds into the video, a man walked right into the camera lens. His eyes were dark and sinister. He walked very close to me and looked at the screen. When he saw what I was filming, he nodded his head and reached for the camera.

Brock instinctively pushed the Mexican man's hand away from me and the camera. I quickly put up my camera thinking the guy wanted to steal it.

I felt the man's breath on my face as he boldly stood inches from me. He stood in between Brock and me.

He pulled out his phone and began speaking quickly and aggressively in Spanish. All of the people who were milling around near the tables stopped moving. The man moving around the shells froze with one hand still cupping a pea. Then, they turned and looked directly at me. Several eyes looked into mine.

Then, the men began to move toward us. They were forming a circle around us.

My face grew hot and perspiration formed on my upper lip. I needed to move, but I felt frozen to the pavement.

Brock whispered, "We've got to get out of here. Follow my lead."

He began to smile and wave his hand. In a strained voice, he said, "Bye, bye! We are leaving!" He looked around at the men surrounding us.

Adrenaline shot through my body as I plastered a smile on my face and waved with my right hand.

Brock began to walk quickly to a store to the right. He went in between a couple of the men, and I followed. Once he got inside the store, he went back out and went toward a store on the opposite side of the sidewalk.

I kept my eyes focused on his back and followed closely as we zigzagged our way back to the place we had entered the market.

We passed a man on the phone. He watched us pass, and then began to follow us.

Another man sitting on a bench, put down his paper, pointed to us after we passed by and then followed us.

I could sense people walking behind us. The road was a few steps away, but then what? There had to be 20 guys on our trail. How could we lose all of them?

I did not dare look behind me. I only looked at the back of Brock's shirt.

When we reached the busy street, Brock grabbed my hand and plunged into traffic.

We ran right in front of a city bus. The bus came to a stop in order to wait for the oncoming traffic to pass so it could turn left.

At this point in time, we ran to the sidewalk on the other side of the street. Now the bus was separating us from the guys in pursuit of us.

Brock yelled, "Run!"

We ran down the street a few blocks back to the warehouse where we had been dropped off earlier. The taxi was no longer there. We didn't pause for long but continued to run for our lives.

We saw a guy pulled over in an empty school bus. Brock began trying to ask in Spanish if he would drive us. The man did not look up from the paper he was reading. He just waved his hand dismissing us.

Across the street, we ran into a clothing store. We ducked behind the clothes on a rack. Before I could talk with Brock about what to do, an American lady with blonde hair entered the store.

Brock ran up to her and said, "Please help us. We're in trouble! Some people are chasing us!"

The lady did not even look at us. She mumbled something about not wanting to get involved. Then, she pointed outside. "There's a policeman. He can help you."

We ran toward the police officer. However, when we reached him, Brock decided not to tell him about what was going on for fear he was in on it. Instead, he asked, "Where is a taxi?"

The policeman pointed to one sitting across the street. We ran over to the cab, but there was no driver to be found. We were in such dire need that the thought crossed my mind to take the car, but there were no keys in it. We continued running.

Brock saw scooters to purchase outside of a store. He thought about borrowing one but dismissed the idea and also realized that they probably did not have gas in them.

We ran a few more blocks and spotted a cab parked on the other side of the street. Brock yelled to the driver standing outside that we needed a ride to the border.

We dove into the backseat. The driver casually sat down and turned on the engine. Brock ducked down so his head was not visible from the window. I did the same but lifted my head a few inches and for the first time since this run began, looked behind me.

There were people out walking along the street. I could not tell if any of them were the ones chasing us.

"If our cab driver gets a phone call, we may have to dive out of this car as it's moving," Brock whispered. "Because that guy back there kept getting on the phone and ordering people to follow us. I don't know exactly what he said, but it seemed like many were in on it. Our driver could be a part of their group."

"What do you think they were going to do?" I asked anxiously as I peered out the side window.

"I think they were trying to kidnap us or worse. It wasn't good, that's for sure!"

I was filled with relief when I saw the border. Brock threw some money at the cabby, and we ran across the bridge to the border checkpoint.

After running several minutes, we were now forced to a complete stop. There was a long line of people in front of us waiting to get into the United States.

Brock said, "If anything happens, you climb over that fence right there." He pointed to the tall fence separating Mexico from the United States. "You will get arrested, but you'll be on the U.S. side."

"Okay," I said breathlessly as I glanced around looking for anyone suspicious.

We nervously waited in the line for 45 minutes. We said nothing to each other. I alternated from looking behind me, to eyeing the fence trying to decide the best way to get over it if I needed to.

When we finally reached the border, I shakily handed my passport to the man at the checkpoint. Would he notice the sweat pouring down my brow? If I looked nervous, he might hold me for questioning.

I glanced over at Brock who was calmly handing his passport to an agent next to me. I envisioned myself getting back over to United States soil and back to my house. I pictured myself sitting out on the back porch watching the birds and squirrels play in the yard. I took a deep breath as I began to slow my heart back to a normal rate.

The man looked from my picture to me and back at my passport. Brock went through and stood on the other side waiting for me.

The agent took one more look at me. "Please let me through," I silently tried to convey with my expression. As the seconds ticked on, I began to get more concerned.

The man smiled and said, "Welcome back!"

Relief flooded through me as I walked through the turn style and joined Brock in the United States. I threw my arms around Brock and held on tight.

Brock was still very tense and looking around on all sides. "Come on. Let's get back to our hotel."

We went to a restaurant close to the venue where the student conference was held. There we talked about what had just happened. Brock called a local guy he had met. We told him what had happened.

"Your ability to sense people around you and act quickly saved your life, my friend," was what he said.

Then, he told Brock about what had recently happened to another local. The drug cartel had taken over Matamoros. This guy had been kidnapped and held by guys with machine guns until he paid them $15,000.

Back at the hotel, Brock got online and did some research. He found out 900 people a day were being kidnapped in the border cities of Mexico at that time. Journalists and people with cameras were being murdered.

"Do you think they were trying to kill us since I was filming them?" I asked. I was sitting on the bed with my feet under the covers leaning my back against the headboard.

Brock sat in an office chair with his laptop laying on the desk. "I'm not sure. I really think they were going to kidnap us for ransom."

A numbness came over me as I said, "I don't want to talk about it anymore."

"Me neither," Brock said closing the computer and climbing in bed next to me. He draped his arm around me and I leaned into his shoulder.

The next couple of days, we went to the conference and performed and Brock spoke. I felt like I was in a fog. I slept, but not very deeply. We did not talk about the incident anymore.

Saturday morning, I woke up in my bed at home. We had arrived late the previous night. I crawled out of bed quietly so as not to wake up Brock.

After putting on shoes, I walked out onto the back porch and looked out onto the hill. The only sounds were the birds chirping.

I breathed in deeply. Here, I felt safe. The only plans we had for the day were to go over to Rod and Susan's house that evening. We had not told anyone what had occurred except a few people at the conference. Maybe we should tell Rod and Susan. Talking about it might help us deal with this dramatic event which took place.

A few minutes later, I took a shower in order to get ready for the day. As the hot water poured over me, I allowed my mind to go back to that scary place in the Mexican market.

Something was familiar about the people in the street stopping and looking at us. "The snakes," I thought. What happened in Mexico was similar to our dream. The man tried to take my camera away and Brock aggressively pushed his hand away like when he threw a rock at the first snake. Then, all of the people stopped what they were doing and stared at us like the many snakes stopped slithering and stared at us.

I quickly toweled off and put on some clothes. Brock was stirring in bed, so I ran over to him.

"What's on your mind?" he asked still groggy from sleep.

"The dreams! I think the snake dreams were about what happened in Mexico!" I blurted out.

Brock began to wake up and we talked about it.

"I think you're right," he concluded. "We have to tell Rod and Susan tonight!"

"I was just thinking that."

****

After eating the burgers Rod had grilled and three-year-old Anna was in bed, the four of us sat together out on the back patio. It was unseasonably cool for July, but the breeze was gentle on my face.

"We think we know what the snake dreams were about," I began.

Brock launched into the story. We told them every detail about what occurred on the streets of Mexico. They stared in amazement as we explained how it correlated with the dream.

"Were you praying the whole time?" Susan asked me.

"Actually, I was only thinking about surviving. I didn't have time to pray, but the good thing is that I've been praying about this situation for the last several months because of the dreams, as have you. This incident had been bathed in prayer before it even began," I said.

"If they did kidnap you for ransom," Susan began, "who would you have called?"

Brock and I looked at each other, but Susan did not let us answer. She said, "You better call us! You were there for me when I didn't even know I needed you. If you ever get into a situation where you need help, I will be offended if you don't call us!"

"Next time we get kidnapped, I promise, we will call you," Brock said with a smile.

This lightened up the night and we all began to snicker a little, except Susan. "I'm serious!" she exclaimed with a fake stern expression.

An interesting look came across Rod's face like something just occurred to him. "What? What are you thinking about?" I asked curiously.

As Rod pulled something up on his iPhone, he said, "You do know what the Mexican flag looks like don't you?"

Then, he turned his phone toward us displaying the flag on the screen. In the center was a large regal bird with a snake in its talon.

Goosebumps rose all over my arms. Susan gasped when she saw the image.

"Now we know the dreams were about Mexico!" Brock exclaimed.

"The Bible study I was reading when I saw the hawks was all about how symbolic God is. Only God could have set this up in the way it happened," I added.

At that moment, we were all so grateful. The Lord had answered our prayers and protected us under the shadow of His wings that day.

Brock began telling the Mexico story in our shows. He shared with the audience that he thought those were really bad men. When Susan offered to pay our ransom, he thought she was a good person. Then, it struck him how wrong he was. He said we tend to think there are good people and bad people. We put ourselves in the good people category, because we know someone worse than we. However, the Bible says in Romans that, "... no one is good, not even one." (Romans 3:10)

He then explained that no matter how much we go to church, or call ourselves a Christian, or give money to the poor, we cannot get to God, because we are separated by our sin. Sin is in our DNA. You don't have to teach a child how to sin. It comes naturally. We are plagued with a disease called sin.

There is only one way to fix our sin problem. A price had to be paid. God sent his only Son, Jesus, to the earth. He lived a perfect, sinless life. Then, they hung Him on a cross and He bled until He died. Three days later, Jesus brought Himself back to life proving that He is the God over all gods, the King over all kings, the Lord over all lords! There is something very special about Jesus Christ.

"If we give our lives to this Jesus," Brock said, "then, and only then, can we have a relationship with Jesus that will ultimately lead to the Father God in heaven."

Every time Brock told the story, I was reminded how involved the Lord was in that whole predicament. He was committed to the details of my life.

My faith was strengthened at this time. I could never have expected that it was about to be put to the test in a huge way as I entered the darkest days of my life.

CHAPTER FIFTEEN
Dying on the Inside

"If I go up to the heavens, You are there; if I make my bed in the depths, You are there. If I rise on the wings of the dawn, if I settle on the far side of the sea, even there Your hand will guide me."
Psalm 139:8-10

I glanced at the time on my phone and realized Brock would be about to wrap up his speaking. I was sitting on a bench outside of the school gym we were performing at this fall day in 2009. This was the seventh school this week.

School shows were a great way to advertise our show that night. We would give them a little taste of what they would see in the big show and Brock would speak about making the right choices with your life. Our hope was that many of them would return for the free show that night and hear the gospel of Jesus. It usually worked very well. The place would be packed with many teenagers and families. They would hear the gospel, and some, the ones who were ready, would surrender their lives to Jesus.

The problem was that I could feel the years being taken off my life when we did them. My day would begin at 6:00 a.m. I would go set up, perform, and tear down three school shows back to back, barely taking time to scarf down some lunch. Then, I would go to the venue for the night performance and begin the four-hour set up. After performing and directing the show, I would tear down our part and finally eat dinner at around 10:00 p.m. The next day, it would begin again, sometimes for three or four days or up to a week. It was brutal.

I looked up into the bright, blue sky and out into the field in front of me. The weather was perfect. I breathed in deeply and let my mind drift.

I thought back over the last few months. Brock and I had just celebrated our tenth wedding anniversary, and we were more in love than ever. We went to Hawaii to celebrate it, which happened to be the fiftieth state that we had visited. I had reached the goal I made when I was in the fifth grade to go to all of the states.

Our ministry was moving along smoothly and the Lord was still working and doing some amazing things. I should have felt completely satisfied with my life. However, something was wrong. It was as if everyone around me was doing life as normal, but someone had hit the mute button when it came to me.

I got up from the bench knowing I needed to go back into the gym in order to play a song we used at the end of our performance. For a brief second, I looked in the opposite direction thinking, "What if I just took off running and didn't come back?"

I shook my head. In all the years doing this ministry, I had never thought this before. In very stressful times, I had told Brock I quit, but was never serious. Brock lovingly teased that I "quit" a couple times a year. This was the first instance I was tempted to do it for real.

Maybe I needed a break. I was so tired all the time lately. A few days ago, I lay down on the bed right when I got into the hotel room. I fell asleep before I had a chance to change into my pajamas or brush my teeth. I slept the entire night in my clothes I had worn in the show. Maybe I could take some time off from the road.

I quickly dismissed the idea. It was impossible for me to miss even one show. Brock needed me there. I was his assistant, production director, stage manager, and whatever else I needed to be. We had to have two people replace me once when I went to visit my family. They still had trouble.

No matter how smart a person was, they didn't have the ten years experience I had. They could not read Brock's expression and know he needed something even though his mouth was going on with the show like normal. They couldn't double check over the tricks to make sure everything was out of the cases and ready to be used. They didn't know which songs to play if the playlist suddenly got out of order, or Brock decided on a whim to go a different direction. I was the only one who could do that.

Although it was comforting knowing I was so essential to this ministry, it was also trapping.

I heard applause coming from the gymnasium. "That's my cue," I mumbled as I drug myself into the room full of high school students cheering at what Brock had said.

As we were loading up, Brock came close to me and asked, "What's wrong?"

I sighed and said, "I'm just tired."

"Tell you what," Brock began with a smile tugging at the corners of his mouth. "When we get home, I'm going to take you on a date."

"You are?" I asked surprised. Since Brock and I were best friends for a while, and then basically decided to get married, we didn't date much before we were married.

The idea of going on an intentional date lifted my spirits a little. "Where are you going to take me?" I asked.

He came closer and whispered in my ear, "It's a surprise."

Goose bumps went down my spine. This idea gave me the energy to finish out the day.

The next few days were a blur and Monday had finally arrived. This was the night we had decided to go on a date. I picked out my favorite outfit and took extra time getting ready. I felt giddy as I put on my makeup.

"You look amazing!" Brock said as I walked into the living room.

"I'm ready to go," I declared.

"Yes, you are," Brock smiled and we headed out the door.

He took me to a fancy restaurant in Nashville we had never been to. Normally we could not afford it. However, Brock had a coupon allowing him 50 percent off.

Brock knew the adventurous spirit in me loved to try new things. Since eating was my hobby, new restaurants were one of my favorite things to experience.

After we had ordered and were already munching on the bread, Brock said, "Tell me about you. What's on your mind?"

"What do you mean?" I asked.

"You don't seem to be yourself lately."

I sighed when Brock said this. If he saw it, there was definitely something wrong with me. I could no longer ignore it.

I began telling him how I felt burned out. I wanted a break but did not see how it was possible.

"Anything's possible," Brock said confidently. "I'll just get John to go with me to the shows, and you take all the time you need."

John was the guy who was working with us at the time. I thought about how quickly he learned and competent he was.

"But John cannot bring you your props onstage or set up the merch table," I argued.

"We will figure it out," he said. "If you need this, then I am going to give it to you."

It was almost October, and our schedule was slim for November and December, so we decided that I could take off the next three months.

The thought of being home for three months made my heart leap! I had not been home without traveling for that long in 15 years. This could be life changing.

I thought of all the possibilities. I could actually have some routine. I could invest in some girls at home. I could write that book I felt like the Lord wanted me to write.

We put our plan into motion. I made plenty of notes for John to use on the road, and I set up a schedule for me at home.

One of my friends I grew up with in Daytona, Tiffany, now lived in a town 30 minutes from my house in Tennessee. She led a woman's Bible study at her church every week. I began attending it, and we would go out to lunch afterward. It was fun to reconnect with her.

There were a couple of other girls I knew that I reconnected with. Also, every Monday that Brock was home was date night. This was what I enjoyed the most.

One day while I was having lunch at a cafe with Tiffany, she looked at me and said, "How do you feel now that you've been home for a month?"

"I enjoy being home, but I am experiencing something that I'm not familiar with."

Tiffany leaned in closer as I continued. "I am having trouble getting out of bed in the mornings. It's so strange because I am a morning person."

"Are you having trouble sleeping?" she asked concerned.

"No, I am sleeping nine hours a night."

"You are probably making up for lost time. Your schedule for the last ten years has been pretty tough."

"Also, I usually look forward to the day when I am showering, but lately I don't look forward to anything."

Tiffany leaned back in her chair and said, "I wonder if you don't feel a sense of purpose. Since you aren't on the road doing the ministry, you feel like you don't have a reason to get up in the morning."

Relief came over me. Tiffany was probably right. This had to be the reason I had been feeling depressed. If I knew the cause, then I could fix the problem. When I got back on the road in January, I would get my purpose along with my passion back.

****

A few days later, when Brock and I were on a date, I told him about Tiffany's and my discussion.

"I think I should give you something to look forward to," Brock said. "Let's go on a trip. We have some time at the beginning of January."

"Where did you have in mind?"

"Let's go out of the country somewhere. I've been talking with Compassion International about meeting the child we sponsor, Bariela, in the Dominican Republic."

"I've heard they have great beaches there," I said picturing myself relaxing on the sand.

"Let's do it!" Brock said excitedly.

"Maybe we could even go over to Haiti and visit Hands and Feet orphanage," I said referring to the orphanage our friend, Mark Stuart, from Audio Adrenaline had founded. "Isn't the Dominican Republic close to Haiti?"

"They share an island," Brock answered. "We've been wanting to go to Haiti. I'll talk to Mark about it."

****

On January 12, 2010, I stretched out on a lawn chair on the sand in Punta Cana on the east end of the Dominican Republic. A gentle breeze off the ocean nipped at the hair around my face. I sighed in contentment. Brock was snorkeling in the water as I read a book on the shore.

Most of the guests at the resort where we were spoke Spanish so I didn't pay any attention to their conversation. However, next to me, I heard the word "tsunami." Without knowing the context, I dismissed it and went back to reading my book.

The next morning, while we were eating breakfast at a restaurant at the resort, I asked Brock why it didn't work out to go to Haiti. We were planning to go to Santa Domingo which was only a two-hour drive to Port Au Prince, Haiti.

"I didn't really pursue it," Brock said nonchalantly.

"Why?" I asked confused. We had wanted to visit Haiti ever since the Party with a Purpose we had to raise money for Hands and Feet.

"I had a bad feeling about it," he answered.

"What do you mean?" I asked.

"I felt the Lord leading us to visit our Compassion child in the Dominican Republic but not to go to Haiti."

"Okay," I said disappointed.

I began to speak again, but Brock held up his finger as if to say be quiet.

"The people at the next table are talking about a tsunami," he whispered.

"I heard people talking about it yesterday, too. Do you think there is going to be a tsunami here?"

"Let's go find out," Brock said drinking the last of his water and standing up.

We had a few minutes before our bus left to take us to Santa Domingo, a city a few hours away. Brock picked up a newspaper which was written in Spanish.

From what we pieced together from the newspaper and a hotel worker's broken English was that Haiti had a big earthquake the day before. Punta Cana was under a tsunami watch.

When we reached Santa Domingo, we went directly to the bed

and breakfast where we would be staying. The owner was very nice and spoke English well. We quickly found out that he was the Belgium Consulate.

He told us that the quake was very devastating from what he had heard. It was a 7.0 on the Richter scale in Haiti but had been a 3.5 in this city where we were.

We were shown to our room where we went online for the first time in several days. I had some emails from family members concerned about us. I reassured them we were okay. Brock looked up more information about the earthquake.

"I guess it's obvious why you had a bad feeling about going to Haiti," I said putting my hand on his shoulder as he stared intently into the computer screen.

****

The next morning, at breakfast, we met Paul, the night manager. He spoke very little English, but was able to communicate some.

We learned he was from Haiti. He and his wife lived in the Dominican Republic, but the rest of his family, including his seven-year-old son, lived in Port Au Prince.

He had not been able to contact them to see if their house was still standing or if they were even alive.

We told him we would be praying.

"Thank you," he said downcast. "Pray that I can get over there to see them. I want to know that my boy is okay."

When we were back up in our room, Brock immediately got back online and began contacting people.

After a few hours, Brock pushed back from the desk where his laptop sat and said, "I want to take Paul and go over to Haiti."

"Well, we are going to meet Bariela tomorrow, but maybe after that, we can both go over there. I'm sure they need all the help they can get," I said.

"It's not going to happen," he said sounding defeated. "Haiti has closed its borders. It would take a miracle for Paul to reach his family right now."

"Let's pray for a miracle for Paul then. It may be months before phones are back up and running. I cannot imagine wondering if your little boy was dead or alive for a few minutes much less weeks!"

****

The next morning, Ivan, our guide who would take us to meet the child we sponsored through Compassion International, picked us up and drove us three hours into the mountains. We found out that Ivan was a former Compassion child. His sponsors lived in Pennsylvania. He now worked for Compassion International.

Ivan told us that the little town where we were going was closer to Haiti and probably had felt the quake much more than they had in Santa Domingo.

"We are here," Ivan said as he parked on a dirt road lined with several small houses. The houses were made of wood with faded blue paint. There were windows and doorways, but no glass or door.

A few adults greeted us at the door and Ivan introduced us to Bariela's parents as well as a few neighbors. When we stepped into the house, Ivan said, "Here she is! This is Bariela!"

A dark-skinned girl with a red shirt and her hair in braids stood shyly inside the house. I walked up to her and got down on my knees so I was eye level with the eight-year-old girl. Then, I gave her a hug.

Brock and I sat on the couch and Bariela sat between us while we gave her a backpack with a few gifts we had brought from the United States. One thing in the backpack was a coloring book and crayons. Bariela immediately sat down on the floor and began to color.

We asked her parents if they had felt the earthquake.

"Oh yes," her father said through Ivan who interpreted. "This house shook so we all ran outside. But, as you can see, the house is still standing."

After talking with Bariela's family for awhile, Brock took out a deck of cards and began doing some tricks. It took a little longer than normal because Brock had to wait for Ivan to translate, but everyone seemed to be impressed.

I noticed neighbors began to come inside and watch Brock. Fifteen minutes later, I counted twenty-two people jammed inside the small house. The two old couches were packed. Some sat on the floor while others stood. Some peered through the windows and doorway to see since there was not any floor space left inside.

"Now, this is community," I thought. It would take us several days of planning to get that many people over to our house. These people came over in a matter of minutes.

Everyone began clapping at an effect Brock had just done. Ivan leaned over and said that we were going to need to be heading back in a few minutes.

"I want to pray for you guys. What do you need?" Brock asked.

I looked over at him, knowing what he was doing. Brock was always looking for a way to meet people's needs. He was fishing for a way to give to them.

Bariela's father said, "Pray for our health and our friends in Haiti."

I asked if they knew anyone in Haiti.

"No, but I know this earthquake is really devastating," was his answer.

My jaw dropped. Guilt washed over me as I realized if Brock asked me the same question, I probably would have had a list of material possessions.

Brock then prayed over Bariela and her community. I felt the presence of the Lord in this tiny house.

As we were leaving, Bariela's father said, "We only want to serve you."

Brock shook his hand and said, "No, we want to serve you."

Bariela's grandmother hugged me tightly and then looked me in the eyes and said, "Blessings."

Tears pricked my eyes as I understood that I was blessed by the few hours spent here more than she knew. I now had a better perspective on life.

I had so much, but wanted more. They had nothing, but were in want of nothing.

****

That night, when we got back to our hotel, Paul greeted us with a smile.

"Did you hear some good news?" Brock asked.

His sister, who lived in Boston, had somehow received news that the house had collapsed but his son was not hurt!

We celebrated with him for this answered prayer.

"Now, I want to go over there to help rebuild the house," he informed us.

Brock told him that he had gone through all of his contacts to try and get him over to Haiti, but they said it was impossible.

We told him we would keep praying he would get to Port Au Prince soon.

****

The following day was our last in the Dominican Republic. Brock and I did some sight seeing around town. At one point, a truck with Haitian license plates and a few guys in the back passed by us. I could see blood dripping out of the bed of the truck.

I was reminded of the tragedy going on down the road. "I wish we could do something," I told Brock.

"Maybe we can. Let's give money to Paul," he said.

"That's a good idea! Back at home, we could give to the Red Cross, but why not give it directly to someone God has put right in our path?"

We found an ATM and retrieved some cash. Then, we went back to our small hotel to find Paul.

He was excited and appreciative. He told us in broken English that he would be going to Haiti the following day.

"How?" Brock asked. "They have closed the borders to everyone."

"My boss is taking me as his security," he said.

"Oh! He's the Belgium Consulate," I said when it registered.

"I guess he is not your average person. I'm so glad that the Lord answered this prayer as well," Brock said excitedly.

We said goodbye and exchanged contact information. We wanted to keep in touch.

On our flight home, Brock and I talked about everything that had happened over the last week. He was grateful God answered our prayers about Paul. He was inspired by our visit to Bariela's house.

"I'm going to take a little nap," I told him as I lay my head against the window.

"Okay," he said. "You rest. I'm too excited to sleep!"

I looked out the window and thought about all the amazing

experiences we had. Brock was exhilarated by it all. However, something was missing with me. I only felt numbness.

"I can't wait to begin doing shows again next week. I need my purpose back," I told myself.

****

My first show back the following week, I was a little nervous, but I got back into the swing of things. When John tried to show me how to pack a new suitcase, I felt anger begin to boil inside of me. I checked my feelings before I blew up at him. Why did I get so mad? Maybe I felt as if I was not needed anymore.

This was not true. Both John and Brock expressed how thankful they were that I was back. So why was I so sensitive? In fact, I had been sensitive about everything lately. Usually, I was not very emotional. However, these days I had been an emotional wreck.

When I wake up in the mornings, I am normally ready to face the world. These days, I could barely get out of bed. I had no energy throughout the day either. Could I possibly be depressed? That could not be it. I was the steady girl, not the moody one. Maybe I was completely burned out with the road...forever.

We kept our date night in place. I began to dump out my feelings on Brock every week.

****

A few weeks later, Brock and I were on a date. He looked across the table of the new Italian restaurant in town and asked me, "How are you feeling now that you are back on the road?"

I broke down in tears. "I thought it would be better, but it's not. I don't feel like myself and I don't know what's wrong with me. I don't think I can do this anymore."

"Do what?" he asked gently.

"Be on the road. I thought that after taking some time off, I would feel refreshed and be ready to begin again, but that's not been the case. I feel worse than before," I explained. Now I was crying so hard it was difficult to breath.

Brock came over to my side of the booth and slipped his arm around me drawing me into his chest. "It's okay," he soothed as he gently stroked my arm. "We will fix it. If you are burned out with this, then we'll do something else."

"You would do that for me?" I looked up at him with surprise. "Change what we are doing?"

"Sure," Brock said with a half smile. "I am not sure what else I can do, but wherever you go, I go."

This warmed my heart to the core. "Let's begin praying about if and what change we should make in our ministry," Brock suggested.

Could I do something else? Would that make me happy again? The thought of this ministry coming to an end sounded devastating, but I did not see any other options.

****

The following morning, I woke up before Brock and went into my usual spot in the living room to spend some time with the Lord. I tried to pray, but felt as if the words were hitting the ceiling. God felt distant. I had not felt His presence or heard from Him in months.

I had been reading my Bible daily since I was in the fifth grade, but for the last several weeks, I had been making excuse after excuse to not read the Word.

Maybe that's the reason the Lord felt so far away. I was not listening to Him by reading His Word.

I picked up my Bible and began reading where I left off. A couple of verses into it, I had to set it down. It was like I did not have the energy to read such a deep book.

"Why is it that I need You the most right now, and You are not here?" I cried into the empty room.

The silence that followed was deafening. I quickly hit "play" on my iTunes list. A song from with the words from Psalm 139 filled the room. My soul started to sooth as I let the lyrics wash over me.

I decided to cling to the promises I had read in scripture. No matter where I go, the Lord is there. He would take care of me no matter what happened. With everything the Lord had done for me, I knew He was trustworthy.

Everything in my life felt muted. It was like life was going on around me but I was not in it. I felt like I was waiting on the side, watching everyone else ride the roller coaster of life. They were all having their ups and downs while I was standing still, going nowhere.

In the past, I was very insensitive when it came to depression. If someone was down, they should just make a change or pull themselves out of the dumps. I was learning that it was not that easy. For once in my life, I felt completely out of control of my emotions, my relationships, my career, my life.

No matter what I did, things became worse. I intended on seeing a counselor, but our schedule was so busy that it was tough to nail down an appointment. Also, I didn't even have the strength to call someone.

Brock began researching new career paths. We investigated moving to Gatlinburg or Las Vegas to do a stationary show. We thought about buying a bed and breakfast in Franklin, Tennessee. We enjoyed hosting and cooking. We could even perform some shows there.

However, our leads did not go far. Nothing felt right.

The thought of starting something new made me exhausted, but continuing the way we were was even more tiring. I did not know what to do.

****

In May, Brock was riding his dirt bike on the track when he had a devastating fall. He broke his back. His T-7 and T-8 were crushed, affecting his breathing, among other things. Although he was not paralyzed and could walk and function, he was in so much pain. I needed to take care of him for the next several weeks. The only problem was that I could barely muster up the energy to take care of myself.

The first week of June, my parents came to visit from Texas. It was great to spend time with them, but I still felt out of sorts. Mom could sense something was not quite in sync with me. She occasionally asked if I was feeling okay.

On Friday of that week, we had my friend, Tiffany, who grew up with me in Florida, and her family coming over for dinner. Brock was on the back porch grilling burgers as I was in the kitchen cooking baked beans.

I began to feel lightheaded as I stood over the stove. Thinking the heat from the oven was getting to me, I went into my room and sat down on the bed.

I took a deep breath and prayed the prayer I had been praying so often lately, "Please, Lord, give me strength."

I stood up so I could get back in the kitchen to finish preparing dinner, but the room began spinning. I felt as if the walls were caving in on me as I collapsed back onto the bed.

Perspiration beaded on my upper lip as I gulped in air. After a few seconds, I began to calm.

I slowly got up again and headed toward the kitchen. After only a few steps, the dizziness returned and I clung to a chair in the dining room.

Then, I tried walking into the kitchen, but I could feel my heart beating in my head. I immediately turned toward the living room and sat on the couch.

What was happening to me? Did this have to do with the anxiety I had lately? Was I having a panic attack?

Mom came into the living room, took one look at my pale complexion and asked, "Are you okay?"

"No," I weakly said. Mom sat beside me and asked what was going on. I explained that I could not walk because I was so dizzy.

At that moment, there was a knock on the door. "Oh no!" I exclaimed. "I'm not done in the kitchen."

"Don't you worry about a thing. I'll take care of it, and Tiffany will understand."

Mom was a great hostess. Of course, she would take over. Also, Tiffany had known me since I was three years old. She would be gracious.

A few minutes later, everyone was crowded around the dining room table eating. "Do you want something to eat?" Mom asked me.

"Just a burger," was my answer.

"No bread or sides?" Mom asked hesitantly.

I shook my head.

"The bread and sides are usually your favorite part," she said with concern. However, she went to retrieve my hamburger for me.

I sat in a chair outside as everyone went on our zip line in the backyard. Mom sat beside me. "How are you feeling now?" she asked.

"I'm fine if I'm sitting down, but when I stand up, the dizziness returns."

My mom was very worried, so she called a friend who worked for a doctor. They discussed my blood sugar and all sorts of things.

Maybe there was something wrong with my health. This might have been something entirely different from the depression I had been feeling. "Now, on top of my fragile emotional state, I have something wrong with me physically," I thought.

We all decided I should get a good night's sleep and hopefully I would feel better in the morning.

As I lay in my bed that night, I tried to go to sleep. I could hear Brock softly snoring next to me. I turned on my side to get more comfortable and felt the bed begin to spin.

"Lord," I whispered. "Am I dying? Honestly, I am ready to die. Let me go be with my Jesus. After all of these months of feeling so horrendous, death would be a welcomed relief."

Eventually, I got still and drifted off to sleep.

In the middle of the night, I woke up feeling my heart beating in my head. The dizziness returned. One thought entered my head, "I am dying."

I began to pray, "Lord, don't let me die! Forget what I said earlier, I want to live!"

That whole night, I tossed and turned convinced that I was close to death.

"How do you feel?" Mom asked when I walked into the kitchen in my pajamas the next morning.

I quickly sat down and the dizziness subsided.

"It was a rough night, but I feel a little better this morning."

She placed her hand on my hair and stroked it. "You take it easy today. I will take care of you. Also, you need to avoid sugar in case your blood sugar is off."

I planted myself on the couch. Mom made me a light breakfast and lunch.

That afternoon, I went to the bathroom. As I walked a few feet, the dizziness violently overtook my body. I reached my hands out in front of me trying to keep my balance.

I picked up my pace and quickly sat down on the toilet.

The dizziness did not subside. The whole room was spinning and then I felt like the walls were closing in on me. My face got hot and I began to sweat. I meagerly called out Brock's name before everything went black.

I woke up on my floor in the bedroom with Brock holding up my head and Mom standing over me. I had thrown up my lunch all over my shirt.

"That's 20 years down the drain," I said with a chuckle.

"What?" Brock said tensely as Mom wiped off my shirt with a towel from the bathroom.

"I haven't thrown up in 20 years!" I said looking at him.

"That doesn't matter! You've been out for a few minutes. We have to get you to the hospital! Can you walk?"

"I think so if someone can help me," I answered sitting up. Mom got on one side and Dad on the other as we slowly inched our way out to the car.

Brock drove as I lay in the backseat with my head in Mom's lap. I could feel the car moving quickly in and out of traffic. Even in my weak state, I giggled as Mom said out loud, "Oh Lord! Don't let us get in a wreck on the way there!"

When we reached the Emergency Room, Dad quickly ran in coming out with a nurse pushing a wheelchair. Mom and Dad helped me onto the chair as Brock ran in to start my paperwork.

They wheeled me up to the desk and I saw Brock speaking with the attendant sitting there. His back was stiff and he clasped his hands nervously. I had never heard Brock sound so uneasy.

Then, I was wheeled into a small room to the right of the entrance desk. A nurse was sitting at a desk with a computer. She swiveled her chair around and looked at me. Frowning, she said, "You look bad."

I glanced at myself in the mirror on the wall to my right. My skin was a pale, pasty yellow. My lips were blue.

"I look dead!" I thought.

The nurse typed some information into her computer and wheeled me into the next room where I was transferred to a bed.

After a few blood tests, a doctor came to the side of the bed.

"Am I dying?" I asked him.

"You are close," the doctor said kindly. "But we are going to give you a blood transfusion and you will feel like a million bucks in the morning!"

"What? I don't understand."

"Young lady, for some reason, you don't have any blood. You are severely anemic. Your iron level should be at about thirteen. You're reading five. Four means you're dead, so it's a good thing you came when you did."

I let the words of the doctor register. I was that low on iron?

The doctor continued, "Iron does not get that low overnight. My guess is that you've been anemic for a very long time. You have probably been feeling awful. Have you noticed a big drop in your energy level over the last few months or maybe even years?"

"Yes, most certainly," was my answer. "I have not felt like myself for months."

"I would say so!" the doctor said with a smile. "You were literally dying inside."

The doctor left and I was in the room by myself. The lack of energy and burn out I was feeling, not wanting to get out of bed in the mornings, everything feeling muted around me, all made sense now.

Relief washed over me. I did not need to find another career! This ministry was not over for me! I just needed blood!

Overnight, they gave me four pints of blood. When I woke the next morning, I looked over at my mom sleeping on a cot in my hospital room. Then, I saw the sunlight peaking in from the window and I felt it!

I could feel the warmth of the Lord. His presence filled the room. He was not muted anymore!

Silent tears trickled down my face as I heard the Lord's comforting words, "*I'm here. I've always been here.*"

A few minutes later, Brock came into the room. He rushed to my bedside and placed his hand on my cheek. Before I could say a word, he whispered, "There's my girl. The girl I married. You have that glimmer back in your smile. It's been missing for awhile."

"Thank you for being so patient with me. I know I wasn't easy to live with lately. No matter how awful I was, you kept me close. I even tried to push you away a few times, but the more I pushed, the closer you came."

Sunlight shone through the window casting light on his face making his blue eyes shine more clearly. As Brock stroked my hair, a thought began to take form. Since I could not hear God, maybe He ministered to me through Brock. The Holy Spirit inside of Brock knew how to take care of me.

"Everybody is asking about you," Brock said. "Rod and Susan, Todd, Ryan, even Barbara has heard about it in Mexico!"

"Wow! News travels quickly," I said.

He took my hand in his and said, "Your color looks so much better."

"I feel so much better," I said smiling.

"The doctor said you need to eat more red meat, and they are going to run some tests to see how you became so anemic, but he thinks it was a crazy, trifecta of things that led to it. The likelihood of this happening again is so slim, but we are going to make sure you get what you need to not get anemic again. Now that we know you're anemic, we can treat it."

He breathed a sigh and looked as if he were going to say something else but changed his mind.

"You know," I began. "All of this would stop if we quit doing shows and telling people about Jesus."

He looked confused and I continued. "The fire and theft and attempted kidnappings and whatever this freaky health issue is all opposition. There is a spiritual war out there and when we tell the gospel to the lost, we are on the front lines. Anyone that shares the message of Jesus takes the chance the enemy will retaliate."

He gave me a vulnerable look as he said, "I know that you are right. Our life has definitely been a roller coaster with many ups and downs. With all of the other things like the fire and brick hitting the windshield, it only made me more passionate about what we are doing. But when I found you passed out, lifeless with no color in your skin, it was the scariest moment of my life."

I placed my hand on his cheek and gently cupped his chin. "You have been strong for the both of us over the last several months, but now I am back!"

"You are?" he asked with a hopeful expression.

"You may feel weary and not as passionate right now but my passion tripled the minute the blood began entering my body. I felt my strength renewed."

At that moment, our roles had reversed. Brock was usually the one giving me the pep talk. However, we had gone through trials before, but this one was the biggest one I had faced. The fire and theft were just possessions. The attempts on our lives were brief. This was a long, difficult attack on my person, but I had made it through! With the

Lord and Brock's help, I was victorious! I felt stronger and more empowered than ever before.

"Well, the people who have booked us for shows in the upcoming weeks are waiting to see if we are going to be able to do them. What do you think?" he asked.

"I think you and I can do anything together," I said quoting him on that night many years ago when we decided to spend the rest of our lives together. Then, I confidently added, "Let's fight on!"

APPENDIX

Brock and me on our wedding day

The bubble car the day we purchased it

Truck moments after the fire was put out (1)

Truck moments after the fire was put out (2)

Our new truck and home combined

We hauled our car in the trailer

Brock grilling on our back porch while parked at Pensacola Beach

Brock's first blind ride in his parents' yard

A Freedom Experience in a high school gym

Brock performing on Fox & Friends at Rockefeller Center in NYC

Brock in the Shower Curtain illusion we performed at Winter Jam